GUATEMALA

MODERN
NATIONS
—OF THE—
WORLD

GUATEMALA

MODERN
NATIONS
—OF THE—
WORLD

GUATEMALA

BY KEVIN DELGADO

LUCENT BOOKS
An imprint of Thomson Gale, a part of The Thomson Corporation

Detroit • New York • San Francisco • San Diego • New Haven, Conn. • Waterville, Maine • London • Munich

On Cover: Guatemala City, Guatemala.

3 1218 00399 4978

© 2005 Thomson Gale, a part of The Thomson Corporation.

Thomson and Star Logo are trademarks and Gale and Lucent Books are registered trademarks used herein under license.

For more information, contact
Lucent Books
27500 Drake Rd.
Farmington Hills, MI 48331-3535
Or you can visit our Internet site at http://www.gale.com

LIBRARY OF CONGRESS CATALOGING-IN-PUBLICATION DATA

Delgado, Kevin, 1971–
    Guatemala / by Kevin Delgado.
       p. cm — (Modern nations of the world)
    Summary: Discusses the geography, history, people, and culture of Guatemala as well as the country's current challenges.
    Includes bibliographical references and index.
       isbn 1-59018-113-1
    1. Guatemala—Juvenile literature. I. Title. II. Series.
       f1463.2.d45 2004
       972.81—dc22
                                                                    2004010557

Printed in the United States of America

CONTENTS

INTRODUCTION
THE LAND OF ETERNAL SPRING

Guatemalans call their country the Land of Eternal Spring. This northernmost Central American country has earned that nickname because of its generally temperate climate year-round. However, the nickname is appropriate for another, less positive reason. Guatemala is a country that has eternally offered a potential that it has yet to fully achieve.

Though theirs is a small country, Guatemalans are a diverse people who claim heritage from many peoples of the world. However, this diversity has long presented challenges for Guatemalans. Though Guatemala is perhaps the home to the best-preserved indigenous culture in all of the Americas, that culture has been brutally repressed. In fact, cultural differences have always been cause for division in Guatemala.

This divisive atmosphere, along with a civil war that lasted more than three decades, has made it difficult for Guatemala to take advantage of its resources and develop as a stable society. Still, the people of Guatemala have remained determined to build a better future for themselves. Though they have endured hardships, they continue to celebrate their culture in their festivals, art, and music. It remains a land of stark contrasts and great potential.

BOUNTIFUL CULTURE
Despite its political and social problems, Guatemala, with its vibrant culture and rich history, fascinates the outside world. Visitors from all over are drawn to its ancient ruins. Perhaps the most famous location in Guatemala is the Mayan ruins at Tikal, the region's leading Mayan city from about A.D. 400–900 located in the northern Petén. This site is an architectural wonder, with its sky-scraping temples and intricately carved stone pillars called stelae.

The Maya of modern-day Guatemala continue to practice many ancient traditions, and most continue to speak their native languages. Though they have clung to their traditions, the Maya have also incorporated certain European elements into their culture. For instance, the indigenous people of Guatemala have blended many aspects of their traditional religion with Catholicism to create a unique hybrid.

The nonindigenous people of Guatemala are known as the ladinos. Many in this group are descendants of the Spanish who colonized the country in the sixteenth and seventeenth centuries. Traditionally this group is more educated than the native Guatemalans and occupies nearly all positions of power in the nation. Not to be overlooked is a distinct society settled along the east coast called the Garífuna. This

GUATEMALA AND
ITS PROVINCES

group is descended from Africans brought to the New World by the slave trade. Today they are mostly subsistence farmers and fishermen who live along the Caribbean coast of Central America from Belize to Nicaragua.

These three groups—the indigenous, the ladinos, and the Garífuna—remain relatively separate and distinct. Though all identify themselves as Guatemalan, each group lives in radically different circumstances and occupies a distinctive niche in the nation's economic and cultural life.

TORTURED HISTORY

As a colony Guatemala was largely marginalized by the Spanish crown, which was more interested in plundering the riches of Mexico and Peru. Consequently the Mayan cultures of what became Guatemala were left relatively untouched by the colonizers.

What evolved in Guatemala as a result was a two-tiered society in which the ruling elite was separate from the indigenous peoples. The ladinos managed to maintain this two-tiered society by relying on dictators who looked out for their interests and enforced laws favorable to them with an iron fist.

In the 1940s and 1950s a popular movement arose that created hope that this pattern of inequity would finally change in Guatemala. Two democratically elected presidents ruled for the ten years between 1944 and 1954. These presidents implemented social reforms aimed at improving the lives of the average Guatemalan. The years that the reforms were enacted came to be known as the Ten Years of Spring. However, unlike the weather in Guatemala, this Spring could not be eternal. Interference from foreign powers resulted in the deposing of the reformers and the reimposition of martial law. The 1954 coup that ousted the democratic government plummeted Guatemala into four decades of bloody civil war. The combatants on one side of this war were right-wing governments backed by Guatemala's landholding elite and anti-Communist paramilitary groups. On the other side were leftist insurgents mostly consisting of indigenous people who demanded the return to the reforms of the Ten Years of Spring. Caught in the middle were rural villagers and anyone who dared to speak out against the government. These people were frequently harassed, tortured, or murdered, or they simply "disappeared."

In 1996 the combatants signed a peace accord, officially ending Guatemala's civil war. However, the war had left some 150,000 people dead, most of them Indian civilians, and some 50,000 missing. The national psyche of the country has still not recovered from the effects of the civil war. As Guatemalans begin the long process of rebuilding, the question of whether this Land of Eternal Spring will finally fulfill its promise remains to be answered.

1

A PLACE WHERE ROOTS RUN DEEP

In 1523 the Spanish conquistador Pedro de Alvarado, fresh from his victory over the Aztecs of central Mexico, traveled south in search of other lands and riches to claim for Spain. What he found was a land of high mountains and nearly impenetrable subtropical rain forests.

The natives Alvarado encountered referred to their land as *Cuauhtemala*, which in Mayan means "Land of Trees." The Spanish translated this word to *Guatemala*, and the name stuck. Upon first glance, this name may seem fitting even today. Subtropical forests cover almost a third of the country. However, Guatemala's landscape is actually much more diverse than is first apparent. From the Atlantic coast to the shores of the Pacific, from the Highlands of the south to the Petén in the north, Guatemala is a patchwork of beautiful and contrasting geographies. In addition to its subtropical forests, Guatemala lays claim to black sand beaches, volcanic peaks, and cactus-studded deserts—all in an area roughly the size of Tennessee.

THE PETÉN

The northern region of Guatemala, sandwiched between Mexico to the west and Belize to the east, is known as the Petén. Part of the Yucatán Peninsula, the Petén is a low limestone plateau that constitutes one-third of the landmass of Guatemala. The generally rainy climate of the Petén is broken only by a short dry season. As a result of sixty-one to sixty-three inches of precipitation a year, the Petén is inhabited by spider monkeys, wild pigs, jaguars, and a variety of exotic birds. Despite the heavy rainfall, few rivers penetrate the Petén. Instead, most of the water seeps through the porous limestone and collects in lakes in underground caverns. These lakes are known as cenotes. The ancient Maya drew from these freshwater reserves for drinking water. Archaeologists have found ceramic pieces and precious stones in these underground lakes, suggesting that the Maya made ceremonial offerings to them.

The Petén is the most sparsely populated and least developed region of Guatemala, but this has not always been the case. Between the years A.D. 250 and A.D. 830, Mayan civilization flourished in the Petén. At the height of Mayan civilization, the region was one of the most densely populated in history: almost 2,600 people per square mile in the cities and up to 1,300 people per square mile in rural areas. By comparison, New York City today has a population density of only 2,300 people per square mile.

By today's standards the land of the Petén is not suitable for farming, and scientists do not fully understand how the Maya managed to support such a large population for so long. What is clear is that beginning around the year 830, the population in the area began to plummet, probably in response to a combination of severe deforestation and drought. Within one hundred years or perhaps even within several decades, two-thirds of the population had disappeared from the Petén. This decline continued for centuries.

During this long decline, the once-ravaged forests regenerated themselves, gradually covering the Mayan temples and other trappings of civilization. Because of the density of the vegetation, the Petén remained virtually inaccessible. In fact, not until 1970 was a road into the region built that could accommodate heavy traffic. Since then, however, the Petén has become one of the fastest-growing regions of Central America. Immigrants now arrive at a rate of three hundred or more a week.

Most of the new arrivals are farmers, loggers, and cattle ranchers who reduce the subtropical forest by as much as 100,000 acres a year. Consequently this area is once again being systematically deforested. Satellite photos taken at the request of the Guatemalan government in the 1980s provide stark evidence of the impact of the new human invasion. "We were startled by what we saw," says Dr. Thomas Sever, an archaeologist with the National Aeronautics and Space Administration's (NASA's) Marshall Space Flight Center. "You often cannot see borders from space because those are just lines on paper. Landsat showed us rain forest up to a line,

*The Maya, who
constructed temples
like this one, ruled
Guatemala's Petén
region for hundreds of
years.*

then tilled land. That was where Mexico stopped and Guatemala began."[1]

What remains of the Petén's rain forest hides many archaeological sites. Of the sites that have been discovered, eighty are considered highly important by archaeologists.

TIKAL

One of these important archeological sites is Tikal, which stands as perhaps the most impressive collection of ancient buildings in Central America. Located in the northeastern region of the Petén, Tikal spans ten square miles and includes temples, plazas, palaces, causeways, and many other structures. Excavation and restoration is a full-time job at Tikal, and although thousands of individual structures have already been unearthed, it is believed that thousands of structures still lie buried in the ground.

In addition to Tikal's importance to archaeologists, the site is of interest to naturalists. Because the government has enforced bans on hunting there since the early 1930s, Tikal is brimming with wildlife. There are nearly three hundred species of birds found in Tikal National Park, including king vultures, crested guans, and ocellated turkeys. The representation of mammal species is almost as impressive, including

THE PRICE OF SLASH-AND-BURN AGRICULTURE

In recent years, people have flocked to the Petén looking to clear a plot of land where they can build a farm. They do this by burning away the forest and exposing what seems to be rich soil. However, despite the lush appearance of the forest, the soil is not inherently fertile. The forest of the Petén is able to regenerate itself only because the rich community of organisms that live there actually creates an ecosystem, a unit that supports itself. By removing the thick foliage, the complex ecosystem that allowed the variety of plants to grow is destroyed. Once this ecosystem is gone, what is left is a mediocre soil for growing crops. After burning the forest, crops can be grown for only a couple of years. The crops deplete the soil of its nutrients, and the sun, no longer blocked out by the forest's canopy, dries out the ground. When this happens, the farmers often move on to burn down another section of the forest.

Slash-and-burn techniques hurt the ecosystem and ruin the landscape.

pumas, jaguars, brocket deer, and black howler monkeys that swing through the treetops. Tikal also boasts 16 species of bats and 350 kinds of butterflies. Few of the animal species in the area pose a serious threat to humans, although notable exceptions include several species of poisonous snakes, such as the fer-de-lance and coral snake.

THE HIGHLANDS

South of the Petén, the central Sierra Madre mountain range, running roughly east and west, cuts across Guatemala. In western and central Guatemala, these mountains form a series of plateaus, high valleys, and more than thirty volcanic cones. Most of these volcanoes are active, and their fiery craters cast a red glow against the night sky. Several are more than 12,000 feet high, including Guatemala's highest peak, Tajumulco, which towers at 13,845 feet above sea level.

Periodic eruptions of Guatemala's volcanoes have produced rich soil that is ideal for growing the region's main crop, coffee. Guatemalan coffee growers employ a method of cultivation that was developed in the late 1800s, one that uses indigenous trees to shade the coffee plants, which need filtered sunlight in order to produce a superior quality of coffee. This method of coffee growing is environmentally friendly, and the farms serve as a habitat for many birds and other animals. Moreover, Guatemalan shade-grown coffee is considered among the finest in the world. In recent years, however, the traditional system has been replaced with methods that require little or no shade in order to improve crop yield. According to writer Robert A. Rice, these new methods "[represent] an attempt to 'technify' the process: What in essence have served as habitats have now become factories."[2]

Residents of the highlands have suffered for their dependence on coffee production. The world coffee market has been flooded with an overabundance of coffee, driving the price down. In 2001 the price of coffee fell by more than half. Faced with such a drastic drop in income, thousands of Guatemalan farmers have become refugees, emigrating to other regions of Guatemala, and even other countries, to find work. Of those who remain, many have required direct food aid. As writer Don Lotter points out, "The loss of jobs [in coffee cultivation] has made the situation much worse. . . .

A Guatemalan farmer plants coffee, the highland region's main crop.

The signs of the coffee crisis can be seen everywhere in the Guatemalan Highlands."[3] Despite the current crisis, coffee continues to be Guatemala's most important export. Other crops cultivated in the highlands include cardamom, corn, cocoa, allspice, and maguey.

GUATEMALA CITY

Even as economic pressures drive many people to move elsewhere, the central highlands remain the most heavily populated of Guatemala's regions. This is also the most industrialized region of Guatemala. This area is responsible for more than half of the country's manufacturing and is home to one-third of the country's citizens. A valley high in the central highlands is the home of Guatemala City, the nation's capital. A modern metropolis, Guatemala City serves as the country's economic and cultural center as well.

Guatemala City was founded on the first day of 1776, after Guatemala's original colonial capital at Antigua was destroyed by a series of devastating earthquakes. For its part, Guatemala City has not been immune to earthquakes. Major temblors have rocked the city on three occasions, most recently in 1976, when an earthquake measuring 7.5 on the Richter scale killed more than twenty thousand people and caused extensive architectural damage.

The greatest challenge for Guatemala City has been rapid population growth driven by difficult economic times in the countryside. The original architects of Guatemala City laid out the settlement in the classical Spanish-style grid around a central plaza. However, the population explosion that the city has experienced since the early 1900s has made highly organized planning and development impossible. As a result the city faces serious shortages of electricity, water, public transportation, police protection, and other necessary services.

As is true elsewhere in Latin America, the contrast between rich and poor is great in Guatemala City. The wealthier residents live in gated suburban communities, while most of the city's middle class live in boxlike houses in the inner city. The native peasants who have migrated from the countryside searching for a better life live in far more primitive conditions in shantytowns consisting of shacks made of plywood, cardboard, or plastic. These communities lack the benefit of clean water supplies or sewage systems. From time to time security forces break up these makeshift camps, though their inhabitants soon return.

THE WESTERN HIGHLANDS
Thirty minutes to the southwest of Guatemala City lies the town of Antigua, which served as Guatemala's capital until a series of earthquakes forced the colonial authority to move government operations to a new site. Today Antigua is a picturesque colonial town with cobblestone streets and the

Agua volcano looming above. Nearby is Lake Atitlán, which British author Aldous Huxley once famously called "the world's most beautiful lake."[4] Three volcanoes flank this lake, and its shores are dotted with a dozen indigenous villages. This area in the mountains west of Guatemala City earns the country its nickname of the Land of the Eternal Spring. The temperature averages sixty degrees Fahrenheit all year long, with a mild climate similar to that of coastal Southern California. Native farmers dominate the area. Though this area

THE MOST BEAUTIFUL LAKE IN THE WORLD

Ninety miles west of Guatemala City lies Lake Atitlán (Nahuatl for "Place of Water"), the most important landmark of the department of Sololé. More than eighty-five thousand years ago, a volcanic eruption wiped out all forms of life from Mexico to Costa Rica, leaving a huge crater. As time went by, the flow of lava from the new volcanoes completely closed the crater. Water levels began to build up inside, and eventually the crater filled with water, creating a lake one thousand feet deep—the deepest lake in the Western Hemisphere. Lake Atitlán sits 5,128 feet above sea level, where its shores are lined with

dozens of indigenous villages, all accessible by boat. When the famous British novelist Aldous Huxley visited Guatemala, he referred to Lake Atitlán as the most beautiful lake in the world. Three spectacular volcanoes—Toliman, Atitlán, and San Pedro—surround the lake. Local wildlife includes dunking ducks, black bass, and spider monkeys.

With depths of one thousand feet, Lake Atitlán is the deepest lake in the Western Hemisphere.

was conquered by the Spanish in the early 1500s, it was largely ignored after that because the mountains failed to yield silver or gold. Because the Spanish left this area alone, the Mayan inhabitants maintained a highly traditional way of life that continues to the present day.

The western highlands are not as biologically diverse as other regions; most of the wildlife here has long since been killed off for food. Only a few foxes, coyotes, squirrels, and other rodents remain. However, bird life in the western highlands remains rich and varied, including migratory North American birds and exotic local birds with brilliant plumage. Among these birds are parrots, macaws, and the quetzal, an iridescent green bird with long, curling tail feathers. Although rare, this bird is the national symbol of Guatemala.

THE VERAPACES

A rare bird, the quetzal is Guatemala's national symbol.

In the pine-covered mountains northeast of the central highlands are the departments (or territories) of Alta Verapaz and

Baja Verapaz. This area was one of the last to be brought under Spanish rule in the sixteenth century. At the time it was
known as the Land of War because the Mayan inhabitants in
the Verapaces, noted for their ferocity, consistently fought all
advances by Spanish conquistadors. Finally, a Spanish friar
named Bartolomé de Las Casas organized a group of Do-
minican monks to pacify the native people by converting
them to Christianity. He was successful in his efforts and re-
named the region *Verapaz*, or "True Peace."

The climate of the Verapaces is generally wet and chilly,
and most of the year it is either rainy or overcast. An average
annual rainfall of nearly seventy inches makes this region
lush and green. The Verapaces are home to several national
treasures, including Semuc Champey, near the town of Lan-
quin, where the Cahabón River cascades over limestone
ledges into a series of still pools. This area is home to a variety of animals, including salamanders, frogs, and many
snakes, in addition to the quetzal.

Until the mid-1970s, there were no paved roads in the Verapaces, and all goods had to be brought into the region by
pack animals along forest roads or by riverboat. An earlier attempt to construct a railroad to the Caribbean was abandoned. However, despite increased economic development
of this region, the Verapaces continues to be the home of
some of Guatemala's poorest residents.

Cobán is the largest city in the western highlands. In the
nineteenth century German immigrants moved in and established vast coffee and cardamom plantations. This era of
German cultural and economic domination lasted until
World War II, when the United States pressed the government of Guatemala to deport the German plantation owners,
many of whom were actively supporting Germany's Nazis.

THE PACIFIC COAST

As the highlands slope south toward the Pacific Ocean, the
climate grows uncomfortably humid and the vegetation is
more tropical. There are no major metropolitan centers
along the two-hundred-mile Pacific coast of Guatemala. The
region is characterized by black volcanic sand beaches on
the coast; mangrove swamps fed by numerous rivers lie just
inland from the beaches. The coast is a fertile plain that
constitutes the country's most important agricultural zone

primarily dedicated to cattle ranching and the growing of sugarcane, cotton, and fruits. On the volcano's slopes, the rich soil is also suitable for growing coffee. Palm trees, the seeds of which are used for oil, grow closer to the coast. Wealthy landowners have established vast plantations along Guatemala's Pacific coast. Indigenous seasonal workers migrate to these plantations from the western highlands, where work is scarce.

The port of San José is the main terminal for most Pacific Ocean commerce; however, Champerico to the north has become home to Guatemala's burgeoning shrimp industry. Red snapper and sardine are also heavily fished in these waters. Other industries along the Pacific coastal plain include petroleum and mining. These industries have polluted Guatemala's Pacific waters and beaches. In recent years, however, residents, along with environmental activists, have obtained from these industries pledges to protect local fish populations as well as a commitment to the restoration of large swaths of mangroves along the coast, which had been illegally logged for years.

THE CARIBBEAN COAST

Unlike the Pacific coast, Guatemala's Caribbean shore has a temperate climate. Along the north coast, the Rio Dulce runs from Lake Izabal, in the eastern part of Guatemala, to the Caribbean Sea. The banks of the Rio Dulce are covered with a variety of flora and populated with exotic birds such as the blue-crowned motmot, the pink-headed warbler, and the white-breasted hawk. Besides being an ecological treasure, the area has a wealth of minerals and precious metals, including gold, silver, chromium, molybdenum, nickel, marble, and jade. The region is covered with forests, mangrove swamps, rivers, and beaches and is totally different from the rest of the country.

The residents of the Caribbean coast are largely of African descent and are known as Garífuna. The Garífuna, descendants of African slaves brought to the Americas in the seventeenth and eighteenth centuries, are culturally distinct from the Maya. In 1795 the African slaves on the island of St. Vincent rebelled and fled to the island of Roatan in Honduras. From there the Garífuna spread out along the Caribbean to Belize, Guatemala, and Honduras, intermarry-

ing with the Maya. As a result of their dual African and Caribbean heritage, the Garífuna have a unique mixture of cultural characteristics that incude circular dances, banana cultivation, and rooster and pig sacrifices. Their ways of food production are still based in subsistence farming and fishing. Despite their numbers on the Caribbean coast, the Garífuna make up less than 1 percent of Guatemala's total population. The Garífuna speak a language that is also called Garífuna, a mixture of French, indigenous languages, Creole, Bambu, and Patua.

A shaman sacrifices a chicken. Religious ceremonies like this one are just one way the Garífuna express their dual culture.

PUERTO BARRIOS
Puerto Barrios is the primary metropolitan area of Guatemala's Caribbean coast. The city lies near an area of extensive banana cultivation. This reflects the fact that the United Fruit Company built Puerto Barrios in the early twentieth century as a port from which to ship its bananas. This powerful American company built a series of railway lines

from the interior to Puerto Barrios. These railways are still used, though the newer, more modern port of Santo Tomés de Castilla now handles much of Guatemala's banana exports. Puerto Barrios remains an important port city. Such products as coffee, fruits, and tropical woods continue to be shipped from there.

The diversity of Guatemala's resources and peoples has made this a fascinating and culturally vibrant nation. Throughout its history, however, Guatemala has been challenged in making the most of those resources. Indeed, often those resources have benefited a small minority whose leaders have exploited the nation's diversity to minimize opposition to their domination of the majority.

A Hidden Wealth

Fresh from their conquest of Mexico, the Spanish arrived in Guatemala in search of more riches. They had heard stories about El Dorado and hoped to find this legendary city of gold. What they found instead was a harsh terrain and a people who, compared to the Aztecs of Mexico, must have seemed utterly primitive. The Spanish, however, had no way of knowing that the natives they encountered were heirs to one of the most advanced civilizations in the world.

The seeming primitiveness of its new subjects and the lack of easily exploited riches would lead Spain to greatly overlook and underappreciate Guatemala. With the mother country expending little effort on dominating Guatemala, much of the country was Spain's colony in name only, much to the advantage of the natives. Whereas the Spanish tried to exterminate native cultures elsewhere, the Maya of Guatemala were left largely alone; a tiny contingent of Spanish formed the basis of a wealthy ruling class. By the twentieth century, Guatemala had become a two-tiered society consisting of a European-oriented upper class and a lower class that clung tightly to its indigenous roots. As a consequence of the inequities inherent in this system, the stage was set for a tragic clash.

THE MAYA

For almost two thousand years, the land that would become Guatemala was home to one of the most advanced civilizations in the ancient world. The people known today as the Maya constructed elaborate cities in the jungles of the highlands and the Petén. From the fourth through the tenth century A.D., a time when Europe was languishing in the Dark Ages, the Maya were using advanced forms of geometry to design structures such as the Great Plaza in Tikal. Mayan mathematicians were able to perform complex calculations that allowed Mayan astronomers to predict with precision the movements of the sun, moon, and planets. Mayan scientists

A modern Mayan priest prays during a religious ceremony. Some ancient Mayan priests acted as kings and were thought to be gods.

developed a calendar more accurate than even the one in general use today. Mayan scholars developed works of art, literature, and philosophy. They developed one of the earliest recorded written languages and set down their history in stone carvings and long paper tablets. They had a highly developed religion that venerated the sun, the moon, and other celestial objects as gods.

The Maya developed farming and irrigation techniques essential for supporting their population. They supplemented this with a vast network of trade. This network was wide, extending north to central Mexico and south into modern-day Panama. Mayan cities as a result were able to flourish across the Central American region.

The Maya did not have a central government but instead employed a system in which priest-kings ruled over individual city-states. These priest-kings were considered divine beings who were entitled to obedience, tribute, and manpower from the people they ruled.

TRANSFORMATION OF THE MAYA

As advanced as Mayan civilization was, by A.D. 950 political strife, civil war, and famine had brought Mayan dominance in the region to an end. Gradually the Maya abandoned their cities to live in small villages. What had once been a highly organized society turned into a system of loosely connected tribes. Toward the end of the thirteenth century, a group of Toltec invaders arrived in Guatemala's Central highlands. They were from the Yucatán and the eastern coast of what is today Mexico. The invaders' numbers were probably small, but their impact radically changed life in the highlands. The relatively peaceful tribes of this area became, under the influence of the Toltecs, aggressive and militaristic. The Toltec established themselves as a political elite, ruling over a series of highland tribes.

The greatest of these tribes were the Quiché, who dominated the central highlands and established their capital, Utatlán, west of what today is the town of Santa Cruz del Quiché. Other tribes included the Kaqchikel, centered around Iximche, north of present-day Antigua; the Tz'utujil, on the slopes of the San Pedro volcano, and the Mam, to the west near the modern-day town of Huehuetenango. A number of smaller tribes controlled the western highlands and the Pacific coast. Although the tribes were culturally linked, they remained politically distinct and disunified.

A DISAPPOINTING CONQUEST

The lack of unity among the Mayan tribes made them an easy target for outsiders to conquer. In the early sixteenth century, with the conquest of the Aztecs in Mexico complete, Hernán Cortés commissioned his deputy commander, Pedro de Alvarado, to bring the area of Guatemala under the control of the Spanish crown. In 1523 Alvarado traveled south along the Pacific coast with 120 horsemen, 300 foot soldiers, and several hundred Mexican Indians. At the time, the area was favorable for conquest. Not only were the tribes disunified, but the highland Mayan population had grown so fast that it had outstripped the food supply, resulting in widespread hunger. Furthermore, the Spanish arrived with enormous military advantages, specifically gunpowder, steel swords, and horses. The Maya fought on foot, with their obsidian-tipped spears and leather shields, and although

they greatly outnumbered Alvarado's modest force, they suffered devastating losses.

By 1525 Alvarado's small force had subdued all the main
highland tribes. First Utatlán was sacked; then the Tz'utujil
were defeated on the shores of Lake Atitlán, followed by the
Pipil, a tribe living along the Pacific coast. Finally, the last of
the major highland tribes, the Mam, were conquered after a
siege of their fortified capital, Zaculeu. Dealing with the
more remote tribes proved more difficult, but by the 1530s
the conquistadors had subdued the vast majority of them.

Confusion characterized the first years of Spanish rule in
Guatemala. The conquistadors had arrived in western
Guatemala with dreams of riches that were based on rumors
of a golden kingdom they called El Dorado. However, the
Quiché capital Utatlán proved to have no riches like those
that the Aztec capital of Tenochtitlán possessed. Not only
were the Maya of the sixteenth century lacking in material
riches, their fragmentary alliances and remote location
made them a difficult people to rule. As one historian points
out, "Native uprisings, Spanish rivalries, and rumors of easy
wealth the next region over created a volatile climate, and Alvarado's impulsive, vicious, and autocratic rule provided little incentive for colonial settlement."[5]

In 1527 Alvarado established the first permanent Spanish
settlement in Guatemala at present-day Ciudad Vieja, at the
foot of the Agua volcano. But Alvarado was restless in the remote city. He had won distinction for his swift subjugation of
the Maya but had not discovered any great stores of gold or
silver. He made other attempts to find riches, including an
expedition to Ecuador and a failed attempt to share in the
booty Francisco Pizarro took from the Inca Empire in Peru.
Eventually Alvarado returned to Mexico, where he died in
1541.

Although Spain's rulers had largely ignored Guatemala
during the years of Alvarado's administration, eventually the
crown decided to make the effort to establish Guatemala as
a viable colony. A corps of royal officials arrived in the highlands soon after Alvarado's death and divided the colony into
administrative districts. The Mayan peoples, who had endured years of pillage, warfare, and population decimation,
were forcibly resettled in *congregaciones* (concentrated populations). The colony might have been officially recognized,

ALVARADO'S LEAP

Pedro de Alvarado had a reputation for trying things others thought were impossible. This reputation was put to the test in 1519 during a battle with the Aztecs. Alvarado found himself cut off from his troops, separated by a waterway many feet wide. Faced with no other option, Alvarado made a running jump dressed in the full armor of a conquistador. Those who were there later swore that the width of the waterway was impossible for a man to jump. Not only that, the water was so deep that a man in armor would surely have drowned trying to cross. According to legend, Alvarado landed safely on the other side in one bound. The feat was so great

that the battle stopped momentarily in awe. This incident later became known as Alvarado's Leap.

Pedro de Alvarado made a daring leap over a wide waterway during a 1519 battle with the Aztecs.

but it was still of little importance. "Yet with little mineral wealth and a shrinking labor force and tribute population, Guatemala, particularly its Western Highlands and Pacific coastal lands, would remain politically and economically marginal,"[6] says historian Greg Grandin.

Thanks to Spain's lack of interest in Guatemala, Mayan culture managed to survive the Spanish conquest. Elsewhere in the Americas, the lure of gold and silver guaranteed intense exploitation by the conquistadors. By contrast, in Guatemala conquistadors could expect only modest rewards for their efforts. In 1570, for example, a crown official described the Guatemalan countryside as a "poor and unfruitful land" where the only commodities in abundance were "corn and chickens"—hardly the stuff of El Dorado. As historian W. George Lovell points out, "Paltry resources in remote terrain often resulted in symbolic Spanish colonization, not obliterating conquest, as was seen in Mexico and Peru."[7]

SPANISH COLONIZATION

Shortly after Alvarado's death, a powerful earthquake struck the Spanish settlement near the Agua volcano. The violent earth movement split Agua's crater and released the lake waters dammed within it. The city was swept away in the resulting flood. In June 1542 the survivors moved to the nearby Panchoy Valley, where they founded the city of Santiago de los Caballeros de Guatemala, today known as Antigua. This colonial city served as the capital of the Audiencia of Guatemala, an area stretching from Chiapas (today's southern Mexico) through what today are the nations of Guatemala, El Salvador, Honduras, Nicaragua, and Costa Rica. The city gradually became somewhat of a cultural center. Central America's first printing press arrived in Antigua in 1660 at the request of the local bishop, Payo Enríquez de Rivera. This press went on to print Bernal Díaz del Castillo's *True Story of the Conquest of New Spain* and the *Guatemalan Gazette*, Central America's first monthly newspaper. Monks from more than thirty orders, including Benedictines and Augustinians, settled in the capital. Spanish architects designed and Indian laborers erected many churches and other buildings. What little wealth the country contained also was concentrated in the capital. For 233 years Antigua would be the third most important city in Latin America, after Mexico City and Lima, Peru.

Antigua's golden age came to an abrupt end on July 29, 1773, when a series of violent earthquakes destroyed a large number of the city's buildings. Surveying the damage, the colonial authorities decided to move the capital one more time to the Valle de la Ermita (Valley of the Hermitage). The new capital known as Nueva Guatemala de la Asunción was officially inaugurated in 1776. This new city, which came to be known simply as Guatemala, or Guatemala City, would continue as the seat of government into the twenty-first century.

The Spanish experienced little if any opposition to their rule in Guatemala and so had no reason to attempt to eradicate the indigenous culture, as they had in Mexico and Peru. Still, for the native inhabitants of Guatemala, life under Spanish rule was harsh. Indians had no rights and were forced to perform hard labor such as building churches and administrative buildings for little or no pay. Diseases brought by the Spanish ravaged the native populations. As historian Lovell points out, "Maya numbers dropped ninety percent or more during the first century of Spanish rule and population recovery was slow and sporadic for centuries thereafter."[8] Periodically, devastating epidemics would descend on the Maya, as illustrated in a letter from a Spanish constable to his superiors in Spain in 1806:

Following colonization by the Spanish, Guatemala thrived during the 1600s and 1700s.

THE DOOMED CAPITAL

Santiago de los Caballeros de Guatemala, or Antigua, as it is known today, is among the oldest cities in the Americas. Central Americans consider it to be among the most beautiful cities in the Americas as well. It was founded as the Guatemalan capital in 1543 after the previous capital was destroyed by a flood. The city was built in the Panchoy Valley, which is surrounded by three volcanoes: Agua, Fuego, and Acatenango. Spanish colonists chose this location because the valley provided a temperate climate and plenty of fertile soil. Antigua quickly became the cultural, economic, religious, political, and educational center for the entire region of Central America. In 1773 Antigua's golden age came to an abrupt end when an earthquake leveled the city, forcing Guatemalans to move their capital once again. The city fell into obscurity throughout the nineteenth and early twentieth centuries. Then, in 1944, Antigua was declared a national monument. Two decades later, Guatemala's congress passed a protective law for Antigua, through which many of the city's historical buildings have been preserved and restored. Religion remains at the center of Antigua culture. The city hosts the largest Lent and Easter celebrations in the Western Hemisphere, with more than fifty processions each year.

We find that most Indian residents have perished and lie unburied all over the place, their decaying corpses eaten by animals which stalk the countryside. . . . After so much hard work, these unfortunate Indians have been reduced to a life of misery. . . . It is a common thing in this parish to encounter Indians, old and dying alike, walking from town to town, from house to house, begging or searching for corn and charity. Others seek loans, leaving as security one of their children, for they have nothing else to offer.[9]

INDEPENDENCE AND MODERNIZATION

While Guatemala's indigenous populations were struggling just to survive and were therefore unable to resist Spanish rule, the ruling class—consisting of Spanish colonists and their descendants—was growing tired of domination by the mother country. Spanish monarchs seemed more interested in the wealth the colony could send their way than in providing any benefits in return. Indeed, by the early nineteenth century, a desire for independence had developed not just in Guatemala but throughout Central America. For a time, the Spanish crown and its colonial representative suppressed any moves toward independence. By 1820, however, the Spanish monarchy, distracted by troubles at home, was in a state of disarray. In the end, Spain granted freedom to Guatemala without a fight.

Despite having Spain's blessing, true independence did not come easily to Guatemala. On September 15, 1821, twelve prominent statesmen signed the Act of Independence of Central America. Mexico's president, Agustin de Iturbide, promptly sent troops to force Guatemala to become part of a Mexican empire. Less than two years later, on June 24, 1823, Guatemala declared independence again. The country then joined in a loose confederation of Central American states called the United Provinces of Central America. These states adopted a constitution modeled on that of the United States. However, internal disagreements tore the United Provinces apart in 1839.

For the next eight years, Guatemala was ruled by a military dictator named José Rafael Carrera Turcios. Then, in an election held in 1847, Carrera was chosen as the nation's president. Seven years later, Carrera was declared president for life. Carrera's rule, which lasted until his death in 1865, set a precedent in Guatemala of the rule of the caudillo, or strongman.

During these years Guatemala remained poor and undeveloped. In 1873 President Justo Rufino Barrios Auyón came to power and set out to develop the nation economically. He initiated land and labor reforms. In addition he helped introduce coffee growing to the country, a move that turned out not to benefit the native peoples. Coffee planters took over Indian lands along the Pacific piedmont and in the Verapaz highlands. These growers demanded that Indian laborers be made available to perform agricultural tasks, and Barrios accommodated them. However, this double plunder of land and labor did not affect all Mayan communities to an equal extent. While in some areas the encroachments of coffee cultivation displaced the tribes that lived there, other communities were spared because their land was situated at elevations that were not favorable to intensive coffee growing.

Justo Rufino Barrios Auyón, who became president in 1873, tried to improve Guatemala's economy.

The descendants of Spanish colonizers, known as ladinos, established large *fincas*, or coffee estates, and Guatemala was soon producing enough coffee to be an important player in the world market. Latin American, African, and Indonesian producers competed to supply buyers in Europe and the United States with low-priced coffee beans. Because of this emphasis on price, the success of any producer depended on the availability of cheap labor. Barrios and the rulers that followed him implemented policies to secure for the farm owners, or *finqueros*, a supply of Indian workers who could be paid little or nothing. Guatemala's army enforced vagrancy laws, debt bondage, and other forms of involuntary servitude to guarantee the labor supply that the country's economy now depended on. The army also saw to it that there would be no opposition to the new social order. As one historian describes it, "To maintain the uneasy truce between the Indian majority and the Spanish-speaking *ladino* shopkeepers, labor contractors, and landlords, soldiers garrisoned towns in the populous regions on the Pacific coast and along the rail line between Guatemala City and the Atlantic port of Puerto Barrios."[10]

JORGE UBICO

As a result of the government's policies, by the beginning of the twentieth century, Guatemala had evolved into a highly stratified society in which a tiny minority of elite coffee growers had gained increasing control over land and labor. Still, economic ruin was an ever-present danger. The country was almost completely dependent on the production of coffee and therefore was subject to the unpredictable changes of international markets. With the onset of the worldwide economic crash known as the Great Depression, which caused financial hardship all over the world, Guatemala's economy nearly collapsed. Economic instability led to social and political unrest, particularly in Guatemala City, where bankruptcies and unemployment were rampant. In 1931 Guatemala's

THE MAYAN CALENDAR

Scholars say that one of the greatest accomplishments of the ancient Maya was the development of an accurate and remarkably complex calendar. The Maya calendar was adopted by the other peoples of Mexico and Central America, such as the Aztecs and the Toltec, who used the mechanics of the calendar unaltered but changed the names of the days of the week and the months. To be able to predict the seasons for farmers and astronomical events for religious rites, Mayan priests used a calendar of two repeating cycles. The Maya believed that time repeated itself in cycles. The first cycle was a 260-day period made up of twenty days that alternated thirteen times before starting again. This cycle was used for religious rituals and astrological predictions. The other cycle was a solar calendar based on the calculation that a year had a little more than 365 days, a more precise system than the calendar we use today. Following the movement of the sun, moon, and stars with such accuracy, the Maya were able to predict such phenomena as eclipses and the spring and autumn equinoxes.

Jorge Ubico (right) is inaugurated in 1931. A representative of wealthy landowners, Ubico ruled Guatemala ruthlessly and efficiently.

ladino elite united to restore order and turned the presidency over to a strongman named Jorge Ubico y Castañeda. He was given virtually unchecked powers to restore social stability and economic growth. Ubico was a ruthless, efficient leader. Upon assuming office, he suspended constitutional freedoms and crushed all opposition, particularly from labor unions. To restore order, he decreed that accused lawbreakers would be harshly punished without first being tried. Utilizing forced labor, Ubico often drafted, from among the ranks of prisoners, workers to construct public buildings, expand road networks, and carry out other public projects. To stabilize the economy, Ubico defended private property and landowners' legal rights to a guaranteed labor supply. Historians Nick Cullather and Piero Gleijeses point out, "[General Ubico] suppressed dissent, legalized the killing of Indians by landlords, enlarged the Army, and organized a personal gestapo."[11] Under Ubico, army generals presided over provincial governments, and army officers staffed state-owned farms, factories, and schools. The social structure of the army resembled that of the *finca:* Eight hundred ladino officers oversaw five thousand Indian soldiers, who slept on the ground, wore ragged uniforms, seldom received pay, and were whipped or shot for small infractions.

Despite the harshness of his policies, Ubico earned great admiration from U.S. investors who found Guatemala to have an ideal business climate. Under Ubico, Guatemala became the principal location for Central American investment for such U.S. businesses as the United Fruit Company and agricultural chemical producer W.R. Grace and Company. For the wealthy upper class, Ubico's policies paid off, as the country saw political order restored and rapid economic growth.

President Ubico's backers believed he had brought Guatemala to the verge of fulfilling its potential as a nation. It had changed from being an underappreciated Spanish colony to the Central American darling of foreign investors. Its economy was becoming modernized and its long-hidden natural resources, such as vast reserves of precious tropical woods, were beginning to be exploited. However, those who opposed Ubico contended that he had built his regime on the backs of the less fortunate through oppressive measures. To these opponents, Guatemala was a place where real progress was still only a distant hope.

3

A PAINFUL COURSE

Midway through the twentieth century, it appeared to many Guatemalans that the country was well on its way to achieving the prosperity the nation had long sought. Political stability had encouraged foreign investment. Although the nation was ruled by a brutal dictator, at least there was peace. That peace, however, would prove short-lived. Guatemalans would soon find themselves in the midst of a brutal civil war.

THE UNITED FRUIT COMPANY

At the beginning of the twentieth century, the United Fruit Company was the largest banana producer in the world. It owned plantations not only in Guatemala but also in Colombia, Costa Rica, Cuba, Jamaica, and Nicaragua. The company also owned 112 miles of railroad linking the plantations with various ports. In 1901, when Guatemala's president Manuel José Estrada Cabrera granted the United Fruit Company the exclusive right to transport mail between Guatemala and the United States, the company got the chance to expand its reach. Eventually, United Fruit's operations would become greater in Guatemala than in any other Latin American country.

The United Fruit Company profited from the absence of democratic institutions in Guatemala. First under President Cabrera, then under President Ubico, United Fruit was given a free hand in expanding its landholdings. The company also received tax exemptions as well as a controlling interest in the country's transport and communications industries. Its huge banana estates occupied hundreds of square miles and employed as many as forty thousand Guatemalans. United Fruit also bought controlling shares in the railroad, electric utility, and telegraph. It administered the nation's only port and controlled both passenger and freight railroad lines.

For its part, Guatemala benefited from the relationship with the United Fruit Company. The company paid its full-time employees high wages, built housing and schools for the children of its employees, and constructed hospitals and research laboratories. The company also sponsored research projects to defeat tropical diseases such as malaria and dengue fever. However, with almost unlimited political influence, the company also reached into every level of government in Guatemala. Company executives determined prices, taxes, and the treatment of workers without interference from the government. With interests in every significant enterprise, United Fruit earned the nickname El Pulpo, "the Octopus."

THE TEN YEARS OF SPRING

By the mid-1940s the economy in Guatemala was enjoying substantial growth, which contributed to the emergence of a small, upwardly mobile middle class. As World War II drew

A worker ambles toward a United Fruit Company building. During the early 1900s, the company exerted great influence over the Guatemalan government.

to a close, the looming defeat of fascism inspired the people of Guatemala to oppose dictatorship; the emergent middle class increasingly demanded political change within the country.

For Jorge Ubico, the beginning of the end came in 1944, when two hundred teachers petitioned him for a wage increase. He not only denied the request but arrested the teachers who had drafted the petition. However, instead of giving up, many additional teachers responded by boycotting the march educators had traditionally held in honor of the president. Ubico then fired anyone who refused to attend the march. Students got involved, organizing a strike and demanding social justice, democracy, and the release of political prisoners. Tensions increased when police suppressed peaceful demonstrations by beating and arresting hundreds of protestors. Far from discouraging the demonstrators, the attacks galvanized resistance to Ubico and made people increasingly willing to risk physical injury and imprisonment to protest his brutal regime. On the morning of June 25, 1944, huge demonstrations outside the National Palace were met by platoons of soldiers, cavalry, tanks, armored cars, machine guns, and police. That afternoon, a group of women conducting a silent procession were fired on by a cavalry troop. Many of the women were wounded, and one—Maria Chincilla Recinos—was killed. This act of repression shocked even those who previously had backed the dictator. Letters and messages demanding his resignation flooded the palace. On July 1, General Ubico resigned his post.

General Federico Ponce Vaides assumed the seat left vacant by Ubico. However, his rule lasted only three months. On October 19, 1944, a group of junior army officers, led by Captain Jacobo Arbenz Guzmán and Major Francisco Javier Arana, ousted Ponce. They also sent Ubico into exile. The rebels' aim was to put Guatemala on the road to freedom. Guatemala's first democratic presidential elections were held in December 1944. Juan José Arévalo Bermejo won the election, receiving 85 percent of the vote. Guatemalan leaders drew up a new constitution that, like the one suspended by Jorge Ubico, guaranteed individual rights. Over the next decade, Guatemala would see unprecedented reforms. This time came to be known as the Ten Years of Spring.

THE 1945 CONSTITUTION

When he assumed the presidency in March 1945, Juan José Arévalo advocated what he termed "spiritual socialism." His goal was to create a capitalist economy while leading a democratic and nationalistic revolution that would benefit the middle and lower classes. In his inaugural speech, he proclaimed that the country would begin a period of sympathy for the common man and woman of Guatemala. This represented a monumental shift in attitude because of the implicit support for Guatemala's indigenous people, a rare gesture for any major political figure to make publicly.

Arévalo's first significant effort on behalf of Guatemala's majority was to sign into law the new constitution. The 1945 constitution contained four primary political reforms. First, it extended voting rights to all men, whether literate or not, and gave the vote to women if they could read and write. The

A Guatamalan student protests against the government. Six decades earlier, protests like this one brought down the regime of Jorge Ubico.

second major provision prohibited the reelection of a sitting president. This provision was meant to ensure that Guatemala would no longer be subjected to rule by dictators who manipulated votes to be elected over and over again. Third, the new constitution required a separation of the military and the government. This too was the result of Arévalo wanting to prevent future presidents from using the army to prop up their regimes. Finally, the 1945 constitution allocated money to the University of San Carlos and granted it autonomy as a tribute to students who had helped overthrow the Ubico regime. The university's autonomy was meant to ensure that intellectuals would have the freedom to counter any future leaders' aspirations for dictatorial powers.

The 1945 constitution sought to protect basic human rights and promote moderate reform. Two of the document's articles had particular significance. Article 91 recognized the right to private property, except under circumstances in which that right might run counter to the national interest. Article 92 narrowed Article 91's interpretation by indicating that the government would be legally empowered to expropriate land at any time to meet the needs of society at large. Although Arévalo never invoked Articles 91 and 92, the existence of these articles alarmed Guatemala's landed elite, who considered them threats to their land holdings. Even after the president purged his government of political extremists in July 1945, large landholders and other political opponents continually accused him of being a Communist.

THE REFORMS OF ARÉVALO

Arévalo did not stop his reformation of Guatemala with the 1945 constitution. Almost immediately, he set about instituting health and social reforms that were aimed at helping poor and working-class individuals. He instituted rural health clinics and projects to pipe in clean water to isolated villages. He backed projects such as the building of much-needed sewage systems in poor neighborhoods. Arévalo also initiated social reforms, such as national literacy programs and farm cooperatives. In 1946 Arévalo began making school reforms aimed at expanding literacy and allocated money for the expansion and improvement of schools. Never before had the Guatemalan government spent so much on the education of all of its people.

In 1947 the Arévalo government enacted a new labor code meant to bridge the gap between the elite minority and poor majority. The labor code for the first time provided workers with the right to strike. Previously, striking workers were punished with torture, imprisonment, and even death. In practice, the labor code did not completely end abuse of strikers by employers, but now those who used violence against strikers could at least be prosecuted. The labor code also set minimum wages, restricted child and female labor, and regulated working hours. Finally, the code created special courts to deal with disputes between labor and management.

In 1947 the Arévalo government also created the Agrarian Studies Commission to evaluate the use and ownership of Guatemala's land and to study how other countries had carried out agrarian reform. This commission was charged with producing recommendations for agrarian reform in Guatemala and investigating the possibility of turning unused land over to peasant farmers. Arévalo's reforms resulted in wage increases, greater social equality, and relative peace in a country that had become accustomed to civil unrest.

A Grab for Power

Arévalo's term was set to come to an end in 1951. Most expected him to be succeeded by one of the two military officers who had become the heroes of the revolution, Jacobo Arbenz Guzmán and Francisco Javier Arana. However, Arana conspired to take power early, and in July 1949 he made his move. With the backing of conservative *finqueros*, he demanded that Arévalo surrender power to the army and serve the remainder of his term as a figurehead for a military regime. In response, Arbenz ordered his troops to arrest Arana on a remote finca. Arana resisted and was killed in a gunfight that followed. Arbenz emerged from this incident a hero to many Guatemalans, since he had saved the country from dictatorship twice over.

In 1950 the people of Guatemala elected Arbenz to succeed Arévalo as the next president of Guatemala. He took office on March 15, 1951. Mindful of the forces that had conspired against him, Arévalo left office with a sense of pessimism for the future of Guatemala. He was well aware

THE CIA IN CENTRAL AMERICA
Just how extensively the U.S. Central Intelligence
Agency was involved in the overthrow of Jacobo Arbenz
Guzmán only came to light in 1997, when activists forced dis-
closure under the Freedom of Information Act. The CIA's Di-
rectorate of Operations compiled lists of prominent
Guatemalan Communists who were to be targeted for assassination. CIA assassination plans included a budget for training
hit teams, target lists, and plans for transferring arms to the
insurgents. The hit lists released were purged of all names, so
who was targeted and what their fate was remain a mystery.
Other proposed tactics included provoking public opinion
against the Communists with fake kidnappings of prominent
citizens and the desecration of churches with graffiti consisting of pro-Communist slogans. Psychological warfare was another CIA tactic. This involved frightening government
officials with death notices and anonymous phone calls early
in the morning. The CIA also used propaganda, which included antigovernment graffiti and phony CIA-written news
articles. In June 1954, under intense pressure from
Guatemala's military, Arbenz stepped down. In Washington,
this confirmed the CIA operation as a success, and the coup
became the model for future CIA actions in Latin America.

that conservative forces of resistance were building
against the revolution from both within and outside of the
country.

A STEP OUT OF LINE
As his predecessor had done, Arbenz announced several reforms focusing on the economy. His first objective was to
make Guatemala's economy less dependent on foreign investors. Second, he announced plans to modernize the
country's economy. Some of the ways he intended to do this
were to build a state-run port to compete with the United
Fruit Company's Puerto Barrios, to reduce the country's re-
liance on United Fruit's railroad by building a highway from
Guatemala City to the Atlantic coast, and to build a national
hydroelectric plant to offer cheaper electricity. All of these
additions to the nation's infrastructure were intended to
raise the standard of living in Guatemala.

Some of Arbenz's most ardent supporters were members of the Guatemalan Labor Party (PGT), as Guatemala's Communist party was known. This support from Communists greatly alarmed the United States. At the time communism was making dramatic inroads in Asia and Eastern Europe. To many Americans, the spread of communism to Latin America seemed a direct threat to the United States itself. Arévalo had been hesitant to work with the Communists for just this reason. Arbenz, however, welcomed their participation.

Jacobo Arbenz was elected president of Guatemala in March 1951 and immediately tried to modernize the country.

Just as alarming to Americans were specific actions by the new president. In late 1951 Arbenz began drawing up land

reform laws intended to make arable land more available to more Guatemalan citizens. At the time, just 2.2 percent of the population owned over 70 percent of the country's land. Furthermore, most of the land was not being used: 90 percent of the population occupied only 10 percent of the land. Arbenz proposed that parcels of land that were in excess of 223 acres be redistributed to peasant farmers. This proposal had international implications, since no entity owned more unused land in Guatemala than the United Fruit Company. The consequences of seizing the holdings of this powerful company were more grave than Arbenz could have anticipated. As early as 1951, the U.S. Central Intelligence Agency (CIA) was already drawing up a contingency plan to oust Arbenz.

On June 17, 1952, the agrarian reform bill containing Arbenz's proposal passed the Guatemalan legislature. For many Guatemalans, this was cause for celebration. The law meant that perhaps thousands of Guatemalans who could never have hoped to own land would now be given the chance to do so. Others understood that there would be severe repercussions for such a bold move. Even some prominent members of the Guatemalan Labor Party had counseled Arbenz against such a dangerous course.

The new law resulted in the expropriation of four-fifths of the United Fruit Company's plantations. In return, the government offered the company $1,185,000 in compensation for land it had valued at $19,350,000. The landed elite lined up on United Fruit's side, making charges that Communists had infiltrated the government of Guatemala.

The United Fruit Company had many important political connections in Washington, D.C. For example, the secretary of state, John Foster Dulles, had represented the company years earlier while working for an influential law firm. The secretary's brother, Allen Dulles, was head of the CIA and had also served on the United Fruit Company's board of directors. Ed Whitman, the company's top public relations officer, was married to President Dwight Eisenhower's private secretary. By 1952, not long after Arbenz's election, the CIA had begun recruiting a force to overthrow him.

In June 1954, the Ten Years of Spring came to an end as anti-Communist insurgents, backed by the CIA, invaded Guatemala from Honduras. In two weeks they had ousted

Arbenz and installed Colonel Carlos Enrique Castillo Armas as the new president. During his term as president, Armas dismantled the progressive reforms set forth by Arévalo and Arbenz. Anticommunism became the guiding principle in the Guatemalan government. The Guatemalan Labor Party was banned, and anyone who opposed this wave of right-wing extremism was condemned as a Communist.

THE SCORCHED EARTH

Political instability and violence followed Armas's coup, culminating in the 1957 assassination of Armas himself. Eventually the legislature appointed General Miguel Ydígoras Fuentes as president. Under Ydígoras, unrest continued, including a peasant rebellion sponsored by Cuba's openly Communist president, Fidel Castro. Ydígoras put down the uprising, and the rebels escaped into the mountains, where they formed the guerrilla group Rebel Armed Forces (FAR).

SEARCHING FOR TRUTH

The rampant violence of the early 1980s caused the international community to finally take notice of the human rights abuses in Guatemala. The first major step came in 1993 with the establishment of a United Nation–brokered Commission for Historical Clarification (CEH). This commission was created to issue an objective assessment of the human rights abuses that had taken place during the thirty-six-year Guatemalan civil war. The commission was to answer questions about why violence had broken out in the first place and to explain why the violence had been used against the civilian population. The CEH was not allowed to reveal the names of those who had committed the atrocities, nor was it given any judicial authority. In February 1999 the CEH issued its final report, a document titled "Memory of Silence." This document was a resolute condemnation of the government's activities during the civil war. The report concluded that though atrocities had been committed by both sides in the civil war, the Guatemalan government had committed acts of genocide against defenseless Mayan communities. It also criticized U.S. companies for promoting an unjust socioeconomic structure and concluded that the U.S. government had constructed and supported structures of repression.

In the wake of the rebellion, the government unleashed a wave of political repression in which it created a blacklist of seventy thousand political suspects—Arbenz sympathizers, members of opposition political parties, and various civilian activist organizations. Thousands of Guatemalans on this list, knowing they faced imprisonment, torture, and death, fled to neighboring countries. Although FAR never numbered more than a few hundred members, the military used the group's existence as rationale for killing thousands of unarmed civilians in its attempts to quash all opposition.

By 1966, however, Guatemalans once again had reason to hope that some measure of political freedom was possible. In March of that year, voters elected Julio César Méndez Montenegro to the presidency. Méndez, a lawyer and university professor, was the first civilian president Guatemala had seen since the ousting of Arbenz in 1954. Moreover, Méndez had openly received the support of the PGT and other opposition parties. However, as the new president prepared to take office, the military stepped in and forced him

 ## THE MURDER OF MYRNA MACK

During Guatemala's civil war, anyone who dared to raise a hand in protest was considered an enemy of the state. Such was the case with Myrna Mack, an anthropologist and a founding member of the Association for the Advancement of Social Sciences. Mack conducted research on the effects of the civil war on rural indigenous communities. Her work drew attention to the serious human rights violations being committed by Guatemala's military. In 1989 she published a study concluding that government counterinsurgency policies had caused the displacement and suffering of Guatemala's indigenous peoples. The study came as peace talks began and was highly damaging to the government. In 1990 members of a military death squad stalked and stabbed Myrna Mack to death. This case was rare only in that the perpetrator of the crime was brought to justice. On October 3, 2002, in a landmark decision, Colonel Juan Vaencia Osorio, an officer of the Presidential High Command, was sentenced to thirty years in prison for ordering the murder of Myrna Mack. However, the vast majority of the state killings that occurred during the civil war remain unsolved and unprosecuted.

to agree not to interfere with its fight against the guerrillas. Furthermore, toward the end of the decade, the legislature exempted the military from following legal procedures when dealing with suspected criminals.

With its military vested with such unchecked power, Guatemala entered a new phase of political repression. No longer were political opponents harassed or arrested; they simply began to disappear. This strategy was so effective that FAR was nearly wiped out by 1970. During that time, thirty-thousand Guatemalans lost their lives and many indigenous people in the Petén, who were unassociated with the insurgency, still were beaten, tortured, raped, or murdered by soldiers, all in the name of fighting insurgents.

Military leaders ruled Guatemala throughout the 1970s, and they continued to wage war against left-wing activists and insurgents, resulting in the deaths of at least 50,000 people during that decade. Army units would routinely attack villages suspected of harboring guerrillas and then slaughter everyone in the village. Virtually any opposition to government policies could bring about a deadly reprisal. One of the most infamous examples of such reprisals occurred on May 29, 1978, when 500 to 700 Mayan Indians from the highlands gathered in Panzós to protest having been evicted from their land. Once the protesters were in the central square, the military surrounded them and opened fire, killing over 100. The soldiers dumped the dead into mass graves. The government later claimed that the Indians had started the violence, a claim made less credible by the fact that the graves had been dug beforehand.

By 1980, the military was targeting students, teachers, unionists, intellectuals, and anyone else who was suspected of opposing the government. People disappeared from mountain villages and from city streets with alarming frequency. Increasingly, rural Indians became targets. In the early 1980s, the army began a campaign called Operación Ceniza (Operation Ashes). In carrying out this campaign, army troops committed mass killings, slaughtered farm animals, and burned villages. This "scorched earth" policy was specifically designed to depopulate areas where guerrillas operated so as to eliminate any potential support for the rebels. Army units killed not just young men, but children, women, and the elderly.

THE PEACE ACCORDS OF 1996

By the end of the 1980s, the Guatemalan government's violations of human rights were drawing international condemnation. In the United States, Guatemala's repressive policies had so outraged voters that U.S. leaders were forced to cut off most military aid. Faced with such significant loss in aid, Guatemala's leaders and the army began to consider negotiating with the guerrillas.

By 1994 the government and the guerrillas had agreed to allow the United Nations to guarantee compliance by both sides with a number of agreements on human rights and demilitarization. With the presence of a United Nations force, state agents, especially members of the military, faced unprecedented limits in their ability to commit violence against government opponents.

The level of violence continued to diminish through the end of 1996, until the rebels and the Guatemalan government signed a final peace accord. What remained was the process of clarifying exactly who did what to whom during this conflict and to hold accountable those responsible for crimes.

For average Guatemalans, the civil war had been a horrific experience that they were not eager to confront. No matter how just the reasons had been for fighting in the first place, most Guatemalans were eager to end the violence and move on with their lives.

CULTURE THROUGH CONTRAST

Guatemala is home to three peoples of distinct origins: the ladinos, who are descended from Spanish colonists; the Garífuna, who are descended from Africans brought to the New World as slaves; and the Maya. Despite economic and social factors that favor integration, daily life in Guatemala reflects and even celebrates the nation's cultural diversity.

MAYA

The Maya are Guatemala's largest ethnic group. The Mayan people are made up of various tribal communities. Each community has its own language and unique folklore. However, they share a common heritage that is expressed in religion, music, dance, and foods. The Maya also maintain customs of dress that set them apart. Most Indian men have adopted some form of Western clothing, though some still wear the *sandalsor*, or sash, and woolen *ponchito*, which identify them as Mayan. Mayan women more commonly wear traditional clothing.

Mayan families tend to be close-knit. Couples tend to marry young and begin having children right away. As a result, Mayan families tend to be large. Most households consist of parents and their unmarried children, though households may include a married son or daughter and their children, as well as elderly in-laws.

The closeness of Mayan families sometimes means that education takes a backseat to helping out at home. Rural children attend small village schools, where they learn basic skills. These children are needed as workers to help support their families. Commonly boys will be pulled from school to go off to work with their fathers, while girls will be kept home to watch younger children and to learn cooking and weaving.

Though the Maya make up the majority in Guatemala, their culture is under almost constant assault. The ladinos tend to see assimilation as the solution to "*el problema del indio*" ("the Indian question"). Indians, in the view of many ladinos, should give up their traditions and adopt ladino ways.

Economic necessity is moving many Maya in the direction of assimilation. As indigenous residents leave their villages in search of work in Guatemala City or in Mexico and the United States, they often adopt non-Indian ways. Those who return to their villages bring the influences of the outside world with them. As a consequence, "small *tiendas* (local stores) are packed with Coca-Cola, Fritos and cigarettes,"[12] says writer Maureen Shea. However, the most significant

Products such as Coca-Cola have become an everyday part of life for the Maya who have moved to the cities.

threat to Mayan culture in modern times was the thirty-seven-year civil war. Right-wing terror groups targeted Mayan villages, particularly in the western highlands, and the vast majority of people who died in that war were Mayan villagers.

Mayan culture, however, has seen somewhat of a resurgence in recent years because of outside influences. For example, there is new interest in Mayan studies programs at universities around the world. Furthermore, Mayan women earn money weaving traditional clothing, which is sold to tourists and even to customers over the Internet. Writer Maureen Shea points out that this new interest is sparking "excitement among the young Mayan population who come into contact with this revitalization movement, and who perceive it as a way to reaffirm their ethnic identity."[13]

The Maya are, for the most part, farmers. Traditionally they view the land as something sacred, something that cannot be owned by an individual. Historian W. George Lovell points out, "Custom dictates that it [land] be worked, protected, and passed on to offspring as a sacred gift handed down from ancestors with that end in mind. Indians consider themselves not so much owners as caretakers of land."[14]

Other traditional ways persist in rural areas. In indigenous communities, most of the women and many men still wear brightly colored native dress. Men usually work the fields, while women care for the children and weave textiles with motifs that are unique to each community. A common diet for a rural family includes corn, beans, and a wide variety of fresh fruits and vegetables. Chicken and rice dishes are also common. Beef or pork is less common among the poorer classes but popular among the middle and upper classes. On festive occasions Guatemalans of all classes serve a variety of native dishes including tamales made from cornmeal that are stuffed with vegetable and meat fillings and wrapped in a banana leaf.

Although during the twentieth century contact with the outside world increased significantly, the homes of rural Indians still look much the way they have for hundreds of years. Such homes are constructed of the materials that are easily available. One common type of housing is a hut made of wooden poles set in a stone foundation. Two doorways are placed directly opposite each other to allow for the free flow of air. The framework is rounded and filled in with additional poles or with stucco. The entire structure is topped by a thick palm-thatched roof. When possible, modern building materials are used to strengthen the basic structure. Examples of modern improvements include cinder blocks and cement for the walls and corrugated metal or tar-and-paper roofing.

GARÍFUNA

In contrast to the Maya, the Garífuna make up a small fraction of Guatemala's, population, less than 2 percent. The Garífuna are a conservative group, devoted to their roots. Theirs is one of the world's few matriarchal societies, meaning that mothers are considered the head of the household. In fact, the Garífuna consider their women to be repositories of cultural wisdom. Tradition also holds that women can communicate with the dead.

This communication is believed to occur in a sacred festival called *dugu*, a word meaning "family reunion," involving relatives both living and deceased. The *dugu* begins with the burning of a fragrant resin, copal, which provides a scent to cleanse the ritual area. Women prepare a feast of fish, conch, and pig. Alcohol is not consumed at all during the *dugu*. Drums are played and women dance until they go into *onwihani*, a trancelike state. Once in this state, they sing messages from ancestors to other family members. Traditionally the Garífuna also believe they can direct the forces of good and evil through spells. These rituals and spells underscore the Garífuna's West African roots. The Garífuna religious system as a whole is a mixture of African and Indian traditions with some elements of Catholicism mixed in. Their religious practices have occasionally drawn accusations of devil worship, polygamy, voodoo, and speaking a secret language, and at times other Guatemalans have feared and discriminated against the Garífuna.

Areas where Garífuna live have little infrastructure, and most people fish or work in the arts. Though Garífuna land is fertile, enough to allow farming, it is mostly the elderly who engage in that occupation. Young Garífuna see no fortune to be made in agriculture and for the most part have dedicated themselves to fishing because the seafood they catch can be immediately sold. There is a small professional

JOURNEY OF THE GARÍFUNA

In 1635 two Spanish ships carrying Nigerian slaves shipwrecked on the island of St. Vincent. The island was already inhabited by a group of people the Spanish referred to as Caribs. The Nigerians made peace with the Carib tribesmen, who allowed the Nigerians to assimilate into their society. Eventually, the two groups intermarried, resulting in black Caribs, also know as Garífuna. In 1776, after warring on the side of the French against the British navy, the Garífuna surrendered control of St. Vincent to England. Because England had designs to develop the island with plantations worked by black slaves, the idea of free blacks living on the island was unacceptable. Therefore, they hunted down and killed hundreds of Garífuna. The British deported those who survived, about 4,300 natives, to another island in the Caribbean, where nearly half died of yellow fever. In 1797 the survivors were transferred once again to the island of Roatan off the coast of Honduras. Later the Spanish captured the island from the British. In the 1830s the Spanish took many Garífuna to Belize to work as woodcutters. The Garífuna prospered and gradually spread down the coast of Central America into Guatemala, Honduras, and Nicaragua. Throughout this time, they maintained unity through language and cultural tradition.

class of teachers, nurses, and civil servants among the Garífuna. However, well-educated people often emigrate to the United States, where they can earn more money. Remittances sent from North America make up a large part of income for many families. Despite this cash infusion, wiring of homes and indoor plumbing are still considered luxuries beyond the means of many Garífuna. Though some live in solid, cement-block houses, the majority live in house-huts that are raised off the ground by stilts to prevent flooding. These huts are constructed of wood with thatched roofs.

In Garífuna society, few couples mark their unions with legal or religious ceremonies. Grandparents often take on the responsibility of raising children. Males generally enjoy permissive boyhoods. However, when they reach manhood, they are expected to leave their mother's house, find jobs, and support their own family. Girls are expected to work at an early age. They are instructed in necessary skills by their mother, grandmother, and aunts. One of the necessities that girls learn is the cooking of traditional Garífuna dishes. These dishes include fish, chicken, pork, corn, coconut, and cassava. In fact, the word *Garífuna* actually means "of the cassava clan." Cassava is a plant harvested for its roots; the roots are boiled and dried into a white meal, which is then used as a flour to make flat bread. Other popular foods include rice, bananas, plantains, and beans.

LADINOS

Though in the minority, ladinos, who refer to themselves simply as Guatemalans, dominate the economic and cultural life in Guatemala. Ladinos are not defined as a specific ethnic group. Most ladinos are of European descent; however, a ladino may also be a full-blooded Indian who has assimilated and adopted ladino culture. Ladinos wear European- and American-style clothing and live mostly in urban areas. Spanish is their primary language.

Ladinos also dominate political life in Guatemala. As one political scientist notes, "The *ladino* ruling class monopolizes the executive, legislative, and judicial branches of the state."[15] In outlying rural areas of the country, ladinos are greatly outnumbered by indigenous residents. However, even in those areas, the ladinos hold a monopoly on positions of influence. They are the mayors and the officers. They own the coffee *fincas* and the banana plantations.

City life in Guatemala—especially in Guatemala City—stands in stark contrast to what is generally found in the outlying areas. Although Guatemala's cities are home to an increasing number of Indians, ladino culture and fashions continue to dominate urban areas. More recently North American culture—including movies, music, business, and even fast-food franchises—have somewhat diminished the predominance of traditional Spanish customs. Though urban ladinos dress in Western-style clothing and speak Spanish, their diet is a blend of both western and indigenous foods: wheat bread and processed foods, on one hand; traditional corn tortillas and rice and beans, on the other.

Well-to-do Guatemalans tend to live in urban centers like Guatemala City, though they commonly maintain residences in the countryside, which they use when they want to get out of the city. Urban residents benefit from the better infrastructure

Life in urban centers such as Guatemala City (pictured) differs greatly from life in rural areas.

that comes with living in a city. Even common amenities such as running water and flushing toilets can be luxuries in some rural areas. Additionally, city dwellers are much more likely to have easier access to professional health care. However, economic differences in urban areas, although not as stark as in the countryside, are great. Therefore, even though urban residents may live near health centers, the poorest segments of the population do not actually have access to the services offered.

Just as access to health care varies by income, so does the availability of good schools. Wealthier families generally send their children to private schools. This is a sign of social status, and some schools are more prestigious than others. Children from families with fewer resources attend public schools. These schools are often overcrowded and lack facilities necessary for a modern education. The poorest children may not attend school at all but instead can be found working as street vendors for little more than the minimum amount of money needed to survive.

Increased urbanization has brought more women into the workforce, creating a demand for child care, especially in urban slums. The poor indigenous women who live in such slums often work as servants in the homes of the well-to-do and middle class. The women often must depend on a government-sponsored day-care program that was launched in 1991 to provide working parents with low-cost child care. This has been a boon to urban women, since almost a quarter of households in the cities are now headed by a female. This is due to many factors, including the abundance of widows as a result of the civil war.

RELIGION

In both urban centers and rural communities, religion plays an important part in daily life in Guatemala. Since the arrival of the Spanish, Guatemala has been an overwhelmingly Catholic country. Before the arrival of the Europeans, though, the indigenous peoples had their own belief systems, based on the natural world and involving the worship of earth and sky deities. Catholic priests in Guatemala have always tolerated the indigenous practice of mixing native and Catholic rituals, and sometimes their own religious practice is mixed in this way. According to Vitalino Simolox, a Presbyterian minister, "I personally know three Catholic priests who privately practice the Maya theology."[16] In fact, at least five thousand native priests currently practice Mayan religious rituals publicly. The trend toward emphasizing Mayan rituals has caused controversy within the Catholic Church's hierarchy in Guatemala over how much divergence from traditional Catholicism should be tolerated. Despite this controversy, the church has continued to reach out to Guatemala's indigenous population. In 1992, the five hundredth anniversary of the Spanish conquest of Guatemala, the Guatemalan Catholic Church issued an apology for abuses committed during the conversion of the Indian population.

In Guatemala the high number of impoverished people has resulted in many Catholics practicing an activist form of their faith that goes beyond the walls of the church. Many of the more affluent parishes have developed projects focusing on the many needs of people living in the outlying areas. These projects tend to focus on issues relating to agricultural production, health education, and the strengthening of local civil society.

As strong as adherence to Catholicism is in Guatemala, since the 1970s evangelical Protestant groups have made substantial gains among churchgoers. As much as 40 percent of the population is now affiliated with some form of Protestantism, primarily evangelical. Protestant churches have historically been less tolerant of the Indian practice of intermixing Christian dogma with pagan symbolism. Some observers claim, however, that the majority of indigenous evangelical churchgoers practice some traditional rituals in private. The success of evangelical sects has contributed to religious diversity, especially in rural areas. "Today it is common to walk into a village in the highland Guatemala and see [many different religious sects right next to each other]. All are in competition with each other. In fact, during prayer, certain formerly quiet towns become quite noisy. Rival houses of worship, sometimes next door to each other, sing as loudly as possible to drown the other out,"[17] says writer Maureen Shea.

Mayan spiritual leaders claim that as much as 50 percent of the indigenous population practices some form of indigenous spiritual ritual, though only around 10 percent do so

Religion is an important part of life in Guatemala. Here people pour out of a church on Good Friday.

openly. Other religious groups that have made gains in Guatemala in recent years include the Church of Jesus Christ of Latter-Day Saints (Mormons) and the Jehovah's Witnesses. Although many Guatemalan residents do not practice any religion actively, very few characterize themselves as atheist.

HOLIDAYS AND FESTIVALS

Despite the increasing diversity in religious practice, Guatemala celebrates traditional Catholic holidays with large public festivals. These celebrations provide citizens with a sense of national belonging as well as a way of affirming one's religious values and customs. Every village and city devotes a celebration to its own patron saint. These days are celebrated with fireworks, music, and processions through the streets. One such large festival is the Feria de Jocotenango (Fair of Jocotenango), held in Guatemala City in honor of the Virgin Mary. This festival originated in the city of Jocotenango, a small town near the old capital of Antigua. However, when the capital was moved to Guatemala City, the Virgin Mary was adopted as the city's patron saint, and the festival was relocated.

Another widely celebrated festival is Carnaval, which constitutes a time of indulgence before the beginning of the Christian season known as Lent. During Carnaval Guatemalans dress in colorful costumes and masks and break colorful, confetti-filled eggshells on the heads of passersby.

Just before Easter Guatemalans work throughout the night to prepare for the most important Christian holiday. Holy Week, the seven days preceding Easter, is commemorated with religious processions, in which images of Jesus and the Virgin Mary are carried through the streets. Antigua, in fact, hosts the largest Easter celebration in the Western Hemisphere. This festival dates back to the 1500s. Some Guatemalans observe Easter in solemn religious earnestness, while others decorate their sidewalks with colorful *alfombras* (carpets), intricate patterns made of flowers, leaves, and colored sawdust.

In Guatemala, school lets out at the end of October and schoolchildren start their vacations from school, which last until early January. The country's temperate weather makes the last months of the year ideal for kite flying, an activity that, in Guatemala, has become associated with cemeteries and the afterlife. Since cemeteries are generally flat and devoid of trees, it has become tradition for children to fly kites in graveyards during the month of November. Folklore holds that this tradition began because kites send messages to the dead. However, according to writer Maureen Shea, the tradition of flying kites during November may have its roots elsewhere. As she points out, "Anthropologist Kenneth W. Smith . . . believes that the practice became a way of attracting single, young women of the town, who were generally inaccessible during most of the year. . . . Flaunting their workmanship and prowess by flying huge kites, the young men attracted attention to themselves and, hopefully gained admiration of desired young women."[18]

THE ART OF THE *ALFOMBRAS*

During the weeklong celebration of Semana Santos (Week of the Saints), which occurs just before Easter, the citizens of Antigua fashion *alfombras*, carpets of brightly colored sand or sawdust, along the parade route. This tradition began when some carpenters spread sawdust to soften the path of the people who carry the heavy floats in the parade. Over the years the tradition has grown to include dozens of brightly colored carpets and many other decorations, such as rose petals or palm leaves. The *alfombras* are short-lived, as they are trampled by people marching in the parade. To begin the *alfombra*, the streets are hosed down, to settle the dust and create a better surface for the carpets. Then wooden forms are placed on the street to contain the sawdust in the desired patterns. Bags of sawdust are then emptied inside the forms and raked flat. Then the artists create a design, starting in the middle of the carpet and working their way outward. Using screened boxes, they sift brightly dyed sawdust into stencils placed on top of the previously laid sawdust. When the patterns are well filled, the wooden forms are removed, leaving a colorful carpet of sawdust on the ground.

A religious procession passes a Guatemalan alfombra, *or carpet, during the Week of the Saints.*

On November 1 Guatemalans celebrate All Saints' Day by engaging in a variety of ceremonies associated with death and the afterlife. Many Guatemalans return to the place of their birth to place flowers, food, and drink at the graves of friends and family members. The next day Guatemalans observe All Souls' Day. The feast held on this day is closely linked to All Saints' Day. However, there is a shift in perspective as the living turn their attention away from the saints in heaven to those sinners whose souls remain in purgatory. According to tradition, this is a day in which souls in purgatory are free to wander among the living. If a household does not provide these souls with offerings of their favorite food and drink, they risk being punished with illness, crop failure, and other disasters.

Just over a month later, on December 7, Guatemalans observe Devil Burning Day by scouring their homes for things that can be thrown away. The trash is burnt in front of each house to purify the home for the Christmas season, which is a time filled with parties and religious observances. During this time, houses are decorated with pine wreaths, poinsettias, and life-sized nativity scenes. On December 8 Guatemalans celebrate the Immaculate Conception, a Spanish tradition popular throughout Latin America. Christmas Eve is celebrated with family and friends. Tamales and punch are traditionally served, and fireworks are set off shortly before midnight. This is when most children open gifts, which have supposedly been brought by the Mary child. The next day, on December 25, family and friends gather around the *nacimiento*, or manger, to sing songs.

These celebrations enrich life in Guatemala. Though life here is filled with stark contrasts, in both lifestyle and religious beliefs, Guatemalans as a people take great pride in their traditions.

5

COLORS AND COMPLEXITY

Perhaps the most recognizable symbol of Guatemala is the colorful patterns of Mayan traditional weavings. However, Guatemala's rich artistic tradition is not limited to textiles. People around the world have come to appreciate many types of Mayan folk art. Furthermore, Garífuna musicians of the Caribbean coast have gained international attention with their brand of Afro-beat music. Guatemala has also been home to many distinguished writers, such as Nobel Prize laureates Miguel Angel Asturias and Rigoberta Menchú Tum. Regardless of the art form or medium in which they work, all of Guatemala's artists and artisans draw inspiration from the nation's rich past and tumultuous present.

TEXTILES

Because of increased international interest in Mayan culture, as well as the sheer beauty of it, Mayan folk art has seen a resurgence since the early 1980s. The brilliant colors and designs of woven Mayan textiles are the most famous form of Guatemalan folk art. Mayan women today continue to express pride in their culture by carrying on this centuries-old craft. Traditionally, Mayan girls begin to learn this intricate and practical craft at a very young age, weaving the colorful fabric on a small backstrap loom. The loom consists of several short sticks that are tied together by a series of vertical cords. One end is usually fastened to a tree or a post, while the other end is wrapped around the weaver's waist. The weaver can therefore adjust the tension of the cords by leaning back. This device was employed by the ancient Maya and can be used nearly anywhere as circumstances allow. Many Mayan women use another type of loom called the treadle loom, which was introduced by Europeans. This large loom consists of a wooden frame and a series of ropes and pulleys that are operated by pedals. The treadle loom can produce large volumes of material in a fraction of the time someone using a backstrap loom would take.

TRAJE

While traditional native dress has been replaced in many parts of the world by popular styles of Western culture, Guatemala remains a place where many indigenous women still proudly wear their traditional dress called *traje*. The style of the *traje* differs between villages and even language groups. Thus, with dozens of Indian towns and villages, and twenty-one Mayan linguistic groups, there is a wide variety of *trajes*. The costumes are made of cotton canvas woven on backstrap looms. They have colorful, abstract patterns using geometric, animal, flower, and other designs. Each design system, along with its associated colors, is so distinctive to a particular village and even to a specific weaver within that village that a person's hometown and familial ties may be determined merely by looking at the style of clothing. This makes the Guatemalan costume truly an expression of cultural identity. The *traje* consists of a *huipil* (blouse) and *corte* (skirt), plus accessories such as a belt or a head wrap. The *huipil* is the most important part of a woman's *traje*. It is constructed of two or three handwoven panels. With rare exception, it is sleeveless with the sides left open. Though there are many styles of *corte*, it is usually sewn together in a tubelike fashion and is worn by stepping into the tube. A complete *traje* can sometimes take months to produce.

Many of Guatemala's Maya proudly wear traje, *or traditional dress.*

No matter which kind of loom is used to produce the fabric, specific color combinations and patterns vary by region. The reason for this is not known, but it is possible that, during the colonial period, Spanish administrators assigned colors and patterns to particular villages in order to keep track of the goods the residents produced. Though at first glance weavings may appear similar, differences in geometric patterns and color schemes hold important regional significance. Specific patterns are associated with a particular village, and as a result local residents can identify where a stranger comes from by the style of his or her garments.

The multicolored dress worn by Mayan women is called a *traje*. It is a combination of a blouse called a *huipil* and a *corte*, which is an ankle-length wraparound skirt. Around the waist, women wear a long sash called a *faja* and usually some sort of headdress or colorful ribbons braided through the hair. The entire ensemble is woven or embroidered and can take months to complete. No two *trajes* are identical. Mayan textiles are popular items in tourist markets. Besides *trajes*, popular woven items include tablecloths, blankets, and napkins.

SANTOS

Trajes are both practical and decorative; another form of folk art, santos, are religious in nature. Santos are wooden figurines carved in the shape of Catholic saints and church leaders. The tradition of the santos goes back to the conquest, when Catholic missionaries needed a way to instruct the indigenous people, who did not know how to read or write Spanish. Indian artisans commonly created wooden representations of their deities, so the missionaries had images of the characters from Bible stories created in similar fashion. Even today many Christians in rural indigenous communities are illiterate and thus cannot read the Scriptures. Santos help them recall the stories of biblical figures whose lives they strive to emulate.

The process of carving and painting a santo can take many days. Sometimes the final coats of paint are applied in the marketplace, creating a work customized to suit the tastes of the buyer. The colors used may also be the same ones found in local weaving patterns. Santos are usually carved out of pine or other woods found locally. The tools are handmade and often made from whatever the woodcarver, or *santero*, could find to get the job done.

MAXIMÓN

Another type of religious folk art particular to Guatemala is a wooden doll called Maximón. Large effigies of Maximón are found in several Guatemalan towns such as Zunil, San Andrés Itzapa, and Santiago Atitlán. The origin of Maximón is unknown, but some cultural anthropologists believe it could be a reincarnation of the Mayan god Mam, who, like Maximón, was represented by a wooden doll dressed in human garb. With the superimposition of Catholicism on indigenous beliefs during the sixteenth and seventeenth centuries, Mam evolved into Saint Simon. However, most of

Maya worshippers make an offering to Maximón, a religious effigy made of wood and found in towns all over Guatemala.

his followers now call him Maximón, a combination of Simon and *max*, the Mayan word for tobacco. Because of this connection to tobacco, Maximón is always represented with a large cigar between his lips. Each Maximón is constructed differently but is always an object of veneration. Visitors from all over the country visit these effigies seeking favors and advice and leave Maximón offerings. According to writer K. Mitchel Snow, "People make offerings to the sinister Maximón . . . to ensure this potentially dangerous saint does not turn against them."[19] To leave him nothing would be a serious offense. Offerings include cigars, tortillas, liquor, and candles.

DANCE MASKS

Just as Maximón draws on both native and Spanish traditions, so too do Guatemalan dance masks. Dance masks originated with the ancient Maya and reflect religious beliefs that predate the Spanish conquest. Like native costumes and languages, dance masks vary from village to village. Regardless of the specific design, the dance masks depict a variety of subjects such as animals, humans, devils, and saints and are made of carved and painted wood or other native materials.

Masks are sometimes incorporated into the process of praying for a good crop or to thank the appropriate saint or god for good fortune. Masks are used to retell a variety of stories, such as the Spanish conquest. The most popular masks are mustached faces representing conquistadors. A common dance including these masks is "Malinche," which tells the story of an Indian woman who betrayed her people by joining up with Hernán Cortés in his conquest of the Aztecs. The masks are carved by skilled craftsmen and artisans and coated with thick, oil-based paint. They are often fitted with painted glass eyes for a lifelike appearance.

LITERATURE

Dance masks are used in retelling events in Guatemala's past, but even more directly reflective of the nation's past political and cultural turmoil is Guatemala's literature. In recent decades Guatemalan literature has gained international attention with the emergence of texts such as *I, Rigoberta Menchú*. This work relates the life of Mayan activist Rigoberta Menchú Tum, whose family perished at the hands of right-wing death squads. The book called international attention to the human rights atrocities committed in Guatemala and led to Menchú winning the Nobel Peace Prize in 1992. As the country deals with its heritage of discord and division, its literature continues to reflect this struggle.

Many Guatemalan literary works look further back, to preconquest times. Although Spaniards burned thousands of Mayan texts in an attempt to wipe out the old religion, myths and partial histories have survived through oral tradition. In addition, archaeologists are beginning to interpret the hieroglyphs carved onto the thousands of stone stelae found in Mayan ruins. Occasionally, too, copies of ancient literary texts surface, providing insights into the history of the Maya. An important example is the *Popol Vuh*, or the *Mayan Book of Counsel.* This is an epic mythology that tells the Mayan story of the creation of mankind. This book might have been lost forever if not for the discovery of a copy in the highlands in the nineteenth century. This version of the *Popol Vuh* had been set to writing in the mid-1600s by rulers in the town of Santa Cruz del Quiché. Since its discovery the *Popol Vuh* has remained in the Guatemalan consciousness and has deeply influenced the country's contemporary literature. Allusions to this mythology can be found in the works of such important Guatemalan writers as Miguel Angel Asturias, Rigoberta Menchú, and Gaspar Pedro González.

Other Mayan documents relate the history of how different tribes waged war on each other and against the Spanish. The *Anales de los Kaqchekles* (*Annals of the Kaqchekeles*) is another important Mayan text. This document, written in the Kaqchekeles language, tells the story of the Spanish invasion from the Mayan perspective. The *Rabinal Achí* relates the story of the struggle between the Rabinal and Gumarcaaj tribes to gain control over the region of Zamneb in the twelfth century. *El libro de Chilam Balam* (*The Book of Chilam Balam*) is yet another Mayan text and recounts the anguish of the Maya as they dealt with the Spanish invasion.

WRITERS OF THE TWENTIETH CENTURY
The work of twentieth-century Guatemalan writers often mirrors the development of Mayan political consciousness.

VOICE OF CHANGE

Rigoberta Menchú Tum was born in 1959 to a poor Quiché family. She became involved in social activism and the women's rights movement while still only a teenager. This activity made her a target among those opposed to the reform movement. Eventually the local militia accused the Menchú family of participating in guerrilla activities. Menchú's father was imprisoned and tortured. After his release, he joined the recently founded Committee of the Peasant Union (CUC). In 1979 Menchú also joined the CUC. Over the next two years, her brother and her father were tortured and murdered by the military. Her mother was also arrested and tortured and died shortly after. In 1981 Menchú fled to Mexico to escape government forces. There she became active in drawing international attention to the atrocities occurring in her homeland. In 1983 she told her life story to Elisabeth Burgos Debray, who committed it to paper in the book *I, Rigoberta Menchú*. Since she left Guatemala, she has returned at least three times to plead for the rights of her people, but death threats have always forced her to return to exile. She has become regarded worldwide as a leading advocate of Indian rights, and her work has earned her several international awards, including the prestigious Nobel Peace Prize in 1992.

Rigoberta Menchú Tum speaks at a 2003 rally.

Early in the century Guatemala saw the emergence of several left-wing writers who came to be known as the Generation of 1920 and 1930. These writers endured censorship and violent repression under the right-wing dictatorships of Manuel Estrada Cabrera and Jorge Ubico. Many of these writers were eventually forced to flee their homeland and live in exile for decades. Many returned to Guatemala after Juan José Arévalo Bermejo assumed the presidency in the 1940s, only to flee the country again when the Ten Years of Spring came to an end. Writers of this era include Miguel Angel Vésquez, Carlos Illescas, Raúl Leiva, Olga Martínez Torres, Melvin René Barahona, and Augusto Monterroso.

During the Ten Years of Spring a new generation of leftist writers arose. These writers used their art to call attention to the inequities that existed in their country between the ladinos and the Maya. However, these writers, including Luis Cardoza y Argón, Mario Monteforte Toledo, and Miguel Angel Astrurias, saw the solution to this problem being the assimilation of the Maya into the ladino culture. Though this view has since been largely disavowed by Guatemala's intellectuals, many of these writers continue to be widely read.

Also during this time a feminist political movement began to grow, primarily within Guatemala's ladino population. The feminists wrote poetry about issues such as abortion and domestic violence. Despite their feminist bent, these writers largely confined their efforts to poetry in keeping with a Latin American tradition that poetry is the domain of women, while the novel is the domain of men. Following this tradition did not, however, necessarily prevent these feminist poets from falling victim to political violence. For example, poet Alaíde Foppa fled to Mexico after the 1954 coup and remained there for many years. Eventually she returned to Guatemala and was kidnapped and murdered by right-wing death squads, becoming a martyr and a symbol of Guatemalan women's resistance to repression.

This attitude of resistance is clearly visible in the work of two notable Mayan poets who came out of the later decades of the twentieth century, Caly Domitila Cane'k and Rigoberta Menchú. Both of these poets were moved to create their work after members of their own families were murdered by right-wing death squads. Caly Domitila Cane'k was a teacher from the northern highlands who wrote in the 1980s in her native Kaqchikel language. Her poetry dealt primarily with the state-sponsored massacres that were leveled upon her village in the late 1970s and 1980s. She eventually fled Guatemala after several of her brothers were murdered. Rigoberta Menchú also wrote testimonial poetry about atrocities committed against her family and members of her village. She began publishing her poetry in the 1990s.

MUSIC

Though until relatively recently Guatemala's literary tradition drew mostly on ladino culture. Guatemala's music draws from a variety of sources. Guatemalan music is rooted in its three cultures: the Maya, the Spanish, and the Garífuna. There are many examples of traditional Mayan music played on the flute, fiddle, or harp. However, the musical instrument that is most closely associated with Guatemala is the

A musician plays traditional music on the marimba, a wooden xylophone native to Guatemala.

IMPORTANCE OF THE MARIMBA

Marimba, the name given to Guatemala's national instrument, means "the wood that sings." This instrument plays a prominent role in Central and South American music. However, in Guatemala, it influences virtually all aspects of life. The music of the marimba can be heard in urban airports, hotels and restaurants, religious services, social processions, and rural traditions. The marimba is considered nothing less than the centerpiece of musical culture. It is evident that music played a very important role in the lives of the ancient Maya as well. Ancient sources such as the *Popol Vuh* describe music being played during accounts of the creation myth and ancestral heroism. But while instruments such as flutes, conch trumpets, and drums are mentioned in ancient texts, it seems that the marimba either did not exist at that time or was not important as a central instrument. Because of the overwhelming national pride invested in the tradition of the marimba, the possibility that it is a nonnative instrument is unthinkable to many Guatemalans. However, there is evidence that the instrument was, at least in part, introduced by outside sources.

marimba, a kind of wooden xylophone. All around the country, during religious ceremonies, parties, and festivals, the marimba is nearly always played. The marimba has become a source of national pride, since many Guatemalans contend that the instrument originated among the Maya before the Spanish conquest. However, many scholars believe that the marimba's origins are in Africa and that African slaves introduced it into Guatemala around 1550. If true, this story suggests that the marimba is most closely associated with the Garífuna culture.

For the Garífuna of the Caribbean coast, music is one of the most important aspects of their culture. Music pervades nearly every aspect of Garífuna life. For instance, the Garífuna play specific music at celebrations of births, observations of deaths, and even public celebrations of the onset of puberty. From a very young age Garífuna children grow up playing instruments made out of discarded household items such as pots, pans, spoons, and matchboxes. Typical Garífuna music builds on an ensemble of three *garaon* drums, suggestive of the artform's African heritage. The Garífuna have modified these drums by adding snares, gut or steel guitar strings, or wires stretched over the drumhead to achieve the buzzing sound. A choir sings and dancers move to create an image of what the lyrics express.

In the 1980s, an era of Latin rock kicked off in Guatemala with the music group Alux Nahual (Quiché for "Spirit of the Goblin"), who fused classic rock music with native traditions. Alux Nahual was the first rock band that put on large-scale concert performance to come out of Central America. Prior to their appearance, public performances were mostly exhibitions put on by popular dance groups; foreign bands dominated the rock music scene. The international success of Alux Nahual has inspired an entire generation of other Guatemalan rock groups who have flourished in the 1990s. Some of the most notable are Bohemia Suburbana, Domestic Fool, Extinción, Fábulas, La Tona, Viento en Contra, Viernes Verde, Malacates Trébol Shop, and Radio Viejo.

ARCHITECTURE

Guatemala's creative spirit, both past and present, is not confined to the fine arts. In both ancient times and since the conquest, artisans have created beautiful structures in Guatemala's rugged landscape. For cen-

turies ancient Mayan cities lay hidden in the jungle, covered by hundreds of years of overgrowth. The techniques the Mayan architects used to build their enormous cities remained a mystery for decades after the cities were uncovered, and archaeologists are still learning.

The ancient Maya built many pyramids throughout Guatemala. Some were sacred and not meant to be touched,

Grand buildings like this one reflect a neoclassical style of architecture that was popular in Europe during the late eighteenth century.

while others were constructed for sacrificial rituals. During these rituals, priests would climb the pyramids along steep stairways that went up the side of the structure. They believed that this brought them closer to the gods. The staircases led from ground level to a temple constructed on top of the pyramid. The temples were relatively small compared to the massive structure of the pyramid. Some temples contained small rooms where high-ranking officials were buried. These chambers often contained treasures such as jade figurines.

Archaeologists speculate that some pyramids served as observatories because of the way they were constructed. For instance a structure might be oriented so that the sun would strike the structure in a certain way only on certain days of the year. Mayan pyramids were most commonly built of limestone, a material found in abundance around most Mayan settlements. Builders worked with simple stone tools such as basalt axes and knives made of obsidian and quartzite.

The Spanish introduced colonial-style architecture to the region with the construction of the cities of Ciudad Vieja and Antigua. Spanish architects drew up the plans for these cities, and native craftsmen constructed the edifices. Indigenous artisans added their own touch to the churches, monasteries, and government buildings they worked on, making them uniquely Guatemalan.

Earthquakes subsequently destroyed most of the colonial buildings of both cities, so relatively few specimens of the colonial era remain. The buildings that have survived in Antigua since colonial times feature elaborate ornamentation typical of sixteenth- and seventeenth-century architecture in Spain. In contrast, Guatemala City was built in the late eighteenth and early nineteenth centuries, and much of the original architecture reflects the much more austere and simple neoclassical style that was popular in Europe at the time.

The architects of Guatemala's capital designed the city to appear similar to a checkerboard, with a main plaza in the middle and four secondary plazas equidistant to the main one. The streets were constructed to run east to west and north to south, radiating from an open square called the Plaza de Armas. The main buildings of the civil and ecclesiastical authorities were placed around this plaza. The socially prominent people built their homes close to this plaza; farther out from the city's center, the mestizo and indigenous population built their houses.

The city has since grown larger and more complex in the years since its founding. Colonial buildings now exist next to modern high-rises, and neighborhoods have become more crowded. Like so much else that is part of Guatemalan heritage, it has adapted to suit a changing reality while holding on to elements of the past.

6

THE ROAD AHEAD

At the beginning of the twenty-first century, Guatemala faces a wide array of difficult challenges. Previously untapped resources are now being exploited, yet the lives of average Guatemalans have not significantly improved. There are, however, signs that better times are ahead. Most Guatemalans regard the 1996 peace accords as offering hope for an end to the country's long and brutal civil war, even though the killing has not ceased. In fact, violent crime is on the rise in Guatemala, much of it reminiscent of the political violence of the past. Furthermore, many of the promises made as part of the peace accords have never been implemented. Guatemala, then, has yet to prove whether the peace accords were truly a watershed event or just a pause in the atrocities.

POLITICS

Most people do not talk openly about what they went through in the 1970s and 1980s, and Guatemalans have yet to put to rest the ghosts of their violent past. This is not merely because those memories are too painful to recall. The danger of those years has not disappeared from Guatemalan society. A stipulation of the 1996 peace agreement was that past atrocities would be investigated and those responsible would be prosecuted. After the agreement was signed, the Catholic Church sponsored a commission to sort through human rights violations. The church published its report under the title "Never Again." Two days after this report came out, the bishop who presented it in the National Cathedral was bludgeoned to death by unknown assailants.

In fact, attacks on human rights workers and other acts of political violence are once again on the rise in Guatemala. Between 2002 and 2004, several Indian leaders and at least one judge were murdered, and many more have been threatened with death. However, instead of being directly linked to the government, these incidents are blamed on highly organized gangs consisting mostly of former death squad members. In 2002 more than seventy complaints were filed with Guatemala's congressionally appointed Office for Human Rights. According to Sergio Morales, who heads up the office, "It is virtually impossible to get to the bottom of such crimes in a nation where less than four percent of criminal complaints ever make it to the courtroom."[20] The government, he says, lacks the will and the resources to deal with human rights violations. To do so would mean confronting not only an ugly past but powerful people as well. Furthermore, several influential government posts are held by officials who have been suspected of past political corruption, making the job of confronting human rights violations even

General Efraín Ríos Montt ruled Guatemala only briefly during the early 1980s but was one of the country's most brutal dictators.

more difficult. Morales has proposed that the government seek help from outside organizations such as the United Nations and Amnesty International. He believes that such international pressure might be enough to stem the violence. Regarding international intervention, however, the administration of outgoing president Alfonso Antonio Portillo Cabrera has said only that the idea should be looked into.

Portillo's position was weakened by the fact that his political party's candidate in the 2003 elections to choose his successor was a former dictator, General José Efraín Ríos Montt. In 1982 Ríos Montt had come to power through a military coup and immediately intensified the government's "scorched earth" policy of murdering indigenous villagers. Though he ruled for only eighteen months, his administration is regarded by many Guatemalans as one of the most brutal in Guatemala's history. For example, under his rule, the military was responsible for killing tens of thousands of Indians and razing around four hundred villages.

In theory Guatemala's constitution barred those who had led coups from running for high office. However, in the summer of 2003 the Guatemalan constitutional court, which was dominated by members of the political party Ríos Montt had founded, ruled that the restriction did not apply to him since he had left office before the constitution took effect in 1983. Therefore Ríos Montt was allowed to run for the presidency.

In November 2003, nearly 80 percent of Guatemalan voters turned out for the presidential election. The campaign centered on wages and crime, two issues important to the indigenous majority. Though no candidate received more than 50 percent of the vote, Ríos Montt placed third, making him ineligible to participate in the runoff election. Ríos Montt opponents had feared that he would steal votes in outlying areas where paramilitary groups that backed him were still strong. To them, therefore, his defeat was a significant victory for democracy in Guatemala. In December, Oscar Berger, a former Guatemala City mayor, was elected to the presidency on the promise of creating a more business-friendly atmosphere in order to encourage foreign investment in Guatemala.

An issue that complicated the election was the presence of hundreds of thousands of former members of paramilitary units. They claimed that the government owed them payment for terror patrols they had performed in the 1970s and 1980s. In May 2003 they burned a southern village and kidnapped its mayor in protest. To placate the paramilitary groups, President Alfonso Portillo announced that the government would pay them what they were owed. This promise only created a problem for the next administration, since the government was already short on cash. However, going back on the promise of back payment would almost certainly prompt more violence. Furthermore, there is no evidence that paying off the paramilitary groups would make them go away.

CRIME

Despite the country's apparent renunciation of political violence, violent crime remains one of the most pressing challenges facing Guatemalans. Nearly sixty people are killed every week in Guatemala City alone—double the murder rate of 2001. This dramatic increase in violence is not only the result of the resurgence of past military leaders and a justice system that investigates only 3 percent of all crime. Guatemala's bloodshed is also the result of growing drug trafficking organizations, an absence of civic leaders (due to the annihilation of standouts during the civil war), and a generation of children orphaned in the civil war who have turned to street crime to survive.

In the countryside, tensions over land distribution and poverty continue to cause problems. These tensions between the landed elite and the poverty-stricken majority have been intensified by Guatemala's struggling economy. In the northern highlands in particular, plummeting coffee prices in recent years have caused the *finqueros* to cut back on the number of workers they employ. This, in turn, has thrown thousands of indigenous laborers out of work. Furthermore, the government has never enacted certain provisions of the 1996 peace accords, which stipulated land distribution and increased social spending.

These problems have allowed the atmosphere of lawlessness to endure in outlying areas, and many of the unemployed have struck back with acts of violence. Groups of Indians occasionally seize at gunpoint the land of large property owners, holding it until the military or private militias evict them. The Indians use the occupation of these lands as a way to draw attention to their causes. However, with neither land nor political representation, the majority of Guatemalans continue to live in virtual serfdom. Wages are kept low because the government has banned trade unions and has denied the use of land for cultivation. Thus the rural population must work as seasonal and migrant laborers. There is a shortage of basic foodstuffs that could be grown on the unused land. Meanwhile, the landed elite enjoy great wealth and political influence.

In the cities a different problem has resulted in increased violence. Guatemala has seen the proliferation of street gangs in urban areas. Many members are youths who emigrated to the United States as children and who were subsequently deported after getting involved in street gang activity in cities such as Los Angeles. They have brought the gang culture with them. Their activity ranges from street fighting to drug dealing. Gang members are easily spotted. Many have shaved heads, baggy pants, and tattoos that advertise

 ## NARCOTRAFFICKING

Guatemala grows only a minimal amount of opium poppy and marijuana. However, the nation remains the preferred Central American country for storage and consolidation of illegal drugs before they are shipped north. Guatemala's long, porous border with Mexico and its central location on the drug route from Columbia make it an ideal center for shipping drugs to the United States and Europe. The U.S. government estimates that up to two hundred metric tons of cocaine are shipped through Guatemala to Mexico and the United States each year. In the early 1990s drug traffickers shipped large amounts of cocaine through Guatemala, using light planes and airstrips carved out of the jungle. This activity was happening on haciendas all over the country, and landowners commonly charged $50,000 per landing. The installation of radar to pinpoint the airstrips has since shifted much of the cocaine traffic onto boats maneuvering along the Atlantic coast. Drug traffickers have also used Guatemala as a storage and packaging base. In 1996, 338 kilograms of cocaine were discovered in a freight hangar at Guatemala City's La Aurora airport. The drug was concealed in suitcases among garments awaiting shipment to Miami.

their gang affiliation. The government is cracking down on these gangs, a policy that is popular with the general public. However, human rights groups fear that this is just one more development that is eroding the nation's civil liberties. The government is considering making all gang activity illegal and punishable with stiff jail terms. However, the government's efforts to discourage gangs continue to be undermined by organized criminals, such as narcotics traffickers, who use gang members to smuggle and deal drugs. Narcotics trafficking is also on the rise in Guatemala, a situation that has allowed gangs to thrive.

Guatemala is primarily a transit point for cocaine that is smuggled to North America from South America. Problems such as corruption and a lack of resources as well as a high turnover rate in law enforcement all continue to thwart Guatemala's efforts to stem the almost constant flow of illegal drugs across its borders.

The amount of illegal drugs passing through the country has contributed to a cycle of misconduct by the police. Guatemalan police officers are poorly paid, and their job is difficult and only getting harder with crime rates on the rise. Furthermore, well-organized drug traffickers often offer bribes to police officers to look the other way, a temptation that is hard to resist when pay is so low.

In fact, in recent years law enforcement has done such a poor job of dealing with the drug problem that in 2003 the U.S. Congress declared that Guatemala was not doing enough to fight the illegal drug trade and removed it from the list of countries the United States deems as allies in the war on drugs. Consequently the United States has cut off certain types of financial aid used for combating drug traffickers. In the four-year presidency of Alfonso Portillo, drug seizure by law enforcement declined by an average of two tons a year. Another significant blow to Guatemala's record came in 2002, when two tons of cocaine disappeared from the warehouses of the national antinarcotics agency. After this incident, three-fourths of the agency's employees were fired on suspicion of corruption.

ECONOMIC DEVELOPMENT

Despite the clear challenges they face, many of Guatemala's indigenous people manage to eke out a living producing and selling goods such as folk art. Demand for Mayan folk art has boomed since the mid-1980s. At least some of these artists have managed to accumulate some savings. These additional resources often lead to more autonomy and local political power because the artists are less dependent on landowners. Because these artists are often women, this has also led to a shift in gender roles in some areas. Though the world market has provided some degree of economic security, folk artists usually stay in their rural areas. However, the children of these folk artists are faced with the dilemma of either continuing the traditions that have been passed down for generations or taking advantage of the increased opportunity that monetary wealth presents.

Like many indigenous people, this Mayan woman makes her living by selling folk arts and crafts.

Far more significant to the nation's economy is the degree to which it has relied on commodities such as coffee and bananas. Though falling prices on these commodities have thrown laborers out of work, the nation's economy grew by 3 percent in 2000 and nearly 4 percent in 2001. This trend is promising, but government officials are still trying to find new ways to expand the economy. Guatemala has recently signed on to the U.S.-proposed Central American Free Trade Agreement, or CAFTA, which would, among other things, open Guatemala's markets to outside competition. The intent of this agreement is to create new outlets for goods already produced in Guatemala as well as to lure new foreign investors to the country. Whether this agreement will be beneficial is controversial. Opponents contend, however, that the agreement will only bring low-wage jobs and foreigners who want to exploit Guatemala's poor.

CHILD LABOR

The precarious state of Guatemala's economy and the low wages people earn as a result mean that children must work to help support their family. Many Mayans start working at a young age. Boys are often put to work on the family farm growing corn. *Finca* laborers often take their sons, who are as young as nine or ten, to the plantation, where they learn to pick coffee beans. Girls usually perform household chores such as taking care of their younger siblings, washing clothes, and preparing food. Girls' chores may also involve learning to weave items to be sold to tourists. Often Mayan girls are sent away to become domestic servants in distant ladino households. Looked upon as second-class citizens, these girls are often subjected to sexual harassment or other forms of physical abuse. In urban areas, young street vendors, selling just about anything they can, risk being run over by cars and also mistreatment by adults. Still more children are subjected to backbreaking labor for little or no pay in areas such as the Baja Verapaz, where youngsters work six days a week making gravel, earning eighteen dollars a month.

According to a 1998 survey by the National Institute of Statistics, there are more than 1 million children in the Guatemalan workforce. Yet despite the efforts of these youngsters, Guatemala has one of the worst hunger problems in Central America because there simply is not enough food to go around. Drought in some areas has reduced crop yields to the point that even if people have money, they find little to buy. Moreover, the weak economy leaves the government unable to help the poorest citizens.

HEALTH SYSTEM

One of the greatest challenges facing the poor in Guatemala is malnutrition and lack of health care. In fact, most Guatemalans have inadequate access to health care because they lack the money to pay for doctors or medicines or because they live in rural areas where health services are minimal. In fact, rural villagers suffer from an 80 percent malnutrition rate and the second highest infant mortality rate in the Western Hemisphere. Rural health problems have been compounded by four decades of civil war, in which millions of Guatemalans have suffered physical and mental trauma. Tragically for Guatemalans, the leading causes of death—pneumonia and influenza, intestinal infections, and malnutrition—are all preventable or highly curable conditions.

Standards of health care tend to differ greatly between urban and rural areas. In cities and large towns, modern state-run hospitals provide health care. Though every small town has a health clinic that provides free services, even the most basic medicines and supplies are often lacking. Furthermore, rural areas present dangers that are not found in the city. Diseases such as malaria, typhus, measles, and dysentery are common and aggravated by poor nutrition. Agricultural laborers also suffer from sicknesses caused by pesticides and fertilizers. In the jungles of the Petén, snakebites are common.

Many rural inhabitants use homemade remedies to treat common ailments, since standardized healthcare is often hard to come by. Still others turn to *curanderos*, or traditional healers. Though they have no formal training in medicine, *curanderos* concoct remedies from local herbs and plants and prescribe them for specific ailments as well as for overall well-being. Some Indians also visit a *zahorin*, a healer who uses charms and prayers to cure illness.

Logistics are always a challenge for health workers in outlying areas. When someone becomes ill in a small community, it can cost a great deal of money to get that person

THE POOREST OF THE POOR

The poorest residents of Guatemala live in and around the city dump in structures made of wood, cardboard, and sheets of corrugated iron. Relief workers estimate that as many as 10,500 people, more than half of whom are children, live this way. They do not have access to education, health care, or even clean drinking water. In order to get by, they scavenge a ravine filled with garbage for recyclable material such as paper, plastic, and cardboard. They in turn sell these items for a meager income. However, this is not enough to live on. Their clothes and much of their food is also scavenged from the dump heaps. The plight of these people has attracted the attention of humanitarian groups and religious missionaries from around the world. However, these groups do not have the resources to keep up with the demand, and as conditions for the poor in Guatemala have not significantly improved, more cardboard houses have gone up around the dump.

to the nearest hospital. The trip often takes several hours, which means that the patient dies of something that need not have been fatal had treatment been more readily available.

DEFORESTATION

Another issue that affects rural residents of Guatemala is deforestation, which is a major environmental problem throughout the Petén and the highlands. This is due in large part to a population boom. For example, the Petén, which had a population of around 20,000 in 1960, in just over forty years has seen its population grow more than twenty-five-fold to over 500,000. As new residents clear the rain forest in order to plant crops, the environmental habitat for countless species of plants and animals continues to shrink or disappear altogether.

Environmentalists say that this clearing of land for farms, along with uncontrolled logging, has created an environmental disaster. Biologists say that because this environment is so unique and isolated, the rain forest may contain species that exist nowhere else in the world. With each square mile of forest that is destroyed, there may be

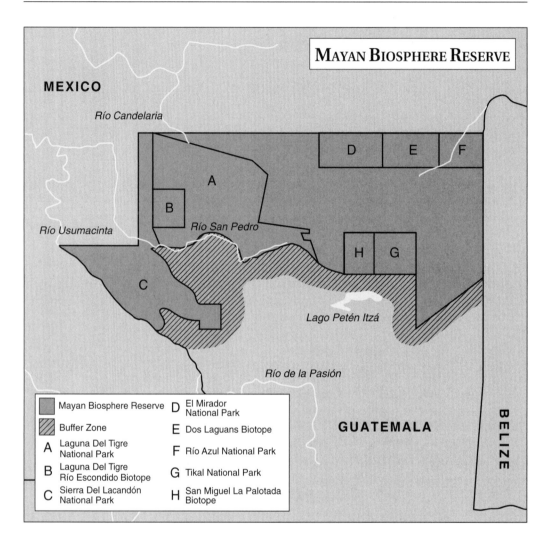

species that are being lost forever before they have even been identified.

The Petén is the chief intact rain forest in Central America. In an attempt to conserve natural biodiversity and stem deforestation, the Guatemalan government established a 4.2-million-acre tract in the Petén in 1990 called the Mayan Biosphere Reserve. Although this marked a new attitude in favor of environmental conservation within Guatemala, deforestation within the Mayan Biosphere Reserve is still widespread. Loggers simply harvest the wood—especially mahogany—and smuggle it across the border to Mexico for sale.

Despite the economic benefits of harvesting, in recent decades Guatemala has paid a high price for clear-cutting its precious wood. As late as the 1980s, the area around the Caribbean Highway east of Guatemala City was an evergreen forest of pine trees. However, in just over twenty years, the practice of clear-cutting has turned it into a desert. Today the area is a barren landscape with exposed soil and only occasional brush and weeds. The most prominent type of plant is cactus.

Guatemala remains at a crossroads. Its people must deal with challenges that have dogged the country for decades and even centuries. Halfway through the twentieth century, the Guatemalan people successfully overthrew a repressive government in a bloodless revolution only to see their country plunged into the bloodiest years of its history only ten years later. Even now, nearly a decade since the signing of the peace accords, that peace is still in jeopardy. Guatemalans must continue to find ways to battle political corruption and foster economic development. At the same time, Guatemala must offer hope for a better life to all of its citizens. Only then can Guatemalans hope that their nation's "eternal spring" will come to fruition.

FACTS ABOUT GUATEMALA

GOVERNMENT

Administrative divisions (22 departments): Alta Verapaz, Baja Verapaz, Chimaltenango, Chiquimula, El Progreso, Escuintla, Guatemala, Huehuetenango, Izabal, Jalapa, Jutiapa, Petén, Quetzaltenango, Quiché, Retalhuleu, Sacatepequez, San Marcos, Santa Rosa, Solola, Suchitepequez, Totonicapan, Zacapa

Capital city: Guatemala City

Constitution: certified on May 31, 1985; effective January 14, 1986 (Suspended May 25, 1993, by former president Jorge Serrano Elías; reinstated June 5, 1993, following ouster of president)

Executive branch cabinet: Council of Ministers, appointed by the president

Chief of state: President Oscar Berger

GEOGRAPHY

Total area: 67,661 sq mi

Climate: hot, humid in lowlands (average annual temperature of 73°–86° F), and cooler in highlands (average annual temperature of 61°–68° F)

Coastline: 249 miles

Highest point: Volcán Tajumulco, 13,846 ft

Lowest point: sea level

Border countries: Belize, El Salvador, Honduras, Mexico

PEOPLE

Total population: 13,314,079 (July 2002 est.)

Population distribution:

    0–14 years: 41.8%

    15–64 years: 54.5%

    65 years and over: 3.7%

Birth rate: 34.17 births/1,000 population (2002 est.)

Death rate: 6.67 deaths/1,000 population (2002 est.)

Ethnic groups: mestizo (mixed Amerindian-Spanish or assimilated

91

Amerindian—in local Spanish called ladino), approximately 55%; Amerindian or predominantly Amerindian, approximately 43%; whites and others, 2%

ECONOMY

Agricultural products: sugarcane, corn, bananas, coffee, beans, cardamom; cattle, sheep, pigs, chickens

Budget:

Expenditures: $2.5 billion

Revenues: $2.1 billion

Currency: quetzal

Notes

Chapter 1: A Place Where Roots Run Deep

1. Quoted in Mark Graffis, "Guatemala May Repeat Mayan History," June 15, 1998. www.hartford-hwp.com/archives/41/205.html.

2. Robert A. Rice, "A Rich Brew from the Shade," *Américas, Organization of American States*, March/April 1998, vol. 50, no. 2, p. 53.

3. Don Lotter, "The Price, Processing and Production Challenges of Growing Coffee Profitably & Sustainably in Guatemala," The New Farm, April 15, 2003. www.newfarm.org/international/guatemala/coffee.shtml.

4. "Lakes," www.enjoyguatemala.com/lakes.htm.

Chapter 2: A Hidden Wealth

5. Greg Grandin, *The Blood of Guatemala: A History of Race and Nation.* Durham, NC: Duke University Press, 2000, p. 26.

6. Grandin, *The Blood of Guatemala*, p. 27.

7. W. George Lovell, *A Beauty That Hurts.* Austin: University of Texas Press, 1995, p. 4.

8. Lovell, *A Beauty That Hurts*, p. 4.

9. Quoted in Lovell, *A Beauty That Hurts*, p. 5.

10. Nick Callather and Piero Gleijeses, *Secret History: The CIA's Classified Account of Its Operations in Guatemala, 1952–1954.* Palo Alto, CA: Stanford University Press, 1999, p. 9.

11. Cullather and Gleijeses, *Secret History*, p. 9.

CHAPTER 4: CULTURE THROUGH CONTRAST

12. Maureen E. Shea, *Culture and Customs of Guatemala,* Westport, CT: Greenwood Press, 2001, p. 52.

13. Shea, *Culture and Customs of Guatemala,* p. 52.

14. Lovell, *A Beauty That Hurts,* p. 6.

15. Edward F. Fischer and R. McKenna Brown, eds., *Maya Cultural Activism in Guatemala.* Austin: University of Texas Press, 1997, p. 24.

16. Quoted in Anita Snow, "Maya Indians No Longer Hide Ancient Faith Behind Catholicism," www.indians.org/welker/maya1.htm.

17. Shea, *Culture and Customs of Guatemala,* p. 35.

18. Shea, *Culture and Customs of Guatemala,* p. 42.

CHAPTER 5: COLORS AND COMPLEXITY

19. K. Mitchel Snow, "Exposing a Heritage in Color & Light," *Américas, Organization of American States,* September/October 1998, vol. 50, no. 5, p. 50.

CHAPTER 6: THE ROAD AHEAD

20. Quoted in Gerry Hadden, "Guatemala Killings Prompt Call for Probe," *Morning Edition,* National Public Radio News, February 7, 2003.

Chronology

2600 B.C.
Maya culture begins in Central America.

300 B.C.–A.D. 1000
Maya culture flourishes in southern Mexico and Central America.

A.D. 600
Construction of Tikal begins.

A.D. 900
Maya begin to abandon Tikal and other major cities.

1290
Toltec-Maya, including Quiché, invade the Guatemalan highlands from the Yucatán and eastern coast of Mexico.

1523
Pedro de Alvarado invades Guatemala with small band of conquistadors and Mexican Indians.

1527
The first permanent Guatemalan capital established at present-day Ciudad Vieja.

1541
Earthquake destroys first Guatemalan capital. Government is moved to Antigua.

1750s
Coffee is introduced into Guatemala.

1773
A series of earthquakes destroy capital at Antigua.

1776
The present capital of Nueva Guatemala de la Asunción (Guatemala City) is officially inaugurated.

1795
Garífuna on the island of St. Vincent rebel and later are transported by the Spanish to Honduras.

1821
Independence from Spain is declared. Act of Independence of Central America is signed in Guatemala City.

1847
United Provinces of Central America dissolves as President Rafael Carrera declares Guatemala an independent state.

1851–1865
José Rafael Carrera Turcios presidency.

1873–1885
Justo Rufino Barrios Auyón presidency.

1898–1920
Manuel José Cabrera Estrada presidency.

1901
President Cabrera grants the United Fruit Company the exclusive right to transport postal mail between Guatemala and the United States.

1931–1944
Jorge Ubico y Castañeda presidency.

1944
President Ubico is deposed in popular uprising known as the October Revolution.

1944–1945
Guatemala governed by a military junta consisting of Francisco Javier Arana, Jacobo Arbenz Guzman, and Jorge Toriello Garrido.

1945–1954
Reform period known as the Ten Years of Spring.

1945–1951
Juan José Arévalo Bermejo presidency.

1951–1954
Jacobo Arbenz Guzmán presidency.

1954
Right-wing insurgents depose President Arbenz in a CIA-backed coup.

1954–1957
Guatemala run by a junta headed first by General Elfego Hernán Monzón Aguirre, then by Carlos Castillo Armas, and finally by Óscar Mendoza Azurdia.

1961–1996
Guatemalan civil war.

1966–1970
Julio César Méndez Montenegro presidency.

1982–1983
José Efraín Ríos Montt presidency.

1996
Peace accords are signed, ending Guatemala's civil war.

2000–2004
Alfonso Antonio Portillo Cabrera presidency.

2001
Price of coffee falls by half on the world market, leading to widespread unemployment.

FOR FURTHER READING

Omar S. Casteneda, *Among the Volcanoes.* New York: Random House Children's, 1992. Young-adult novel about a young Mayan girl and her ill mother. Deals with issues of how the people of this culture struggle to exist in the contemporary world.

Kristine L. Franklin, *Out of the Dump: Writings and Photographs by Children from Guatemala.* New York: HarperCollins Children's, 1996. A sobering account of the hundreds of children who spend their days scavenging through Guatemala City's central garbage dump, searching for items to recycle or resell.

Gerry Hadden, *Teenage Refugees from Guatemala Speak Out.* New York: Rosen, 1997. Personal narratives by young Guatemalan people, who recall memories of their homeland, families, and friends left behind.

Alberto Ruiz De Larramendi, *Tropical Rain Forests of Central America.* New York: Scholastic Library, 1993. This text is a comprehensive guide to the plants, animals, and tribes of the tropical rain forests of Central America.

James D. Sexton, *Mayan Folktales: Folklore from Lake Atitlan, Guatemala.* Albuquerque: University of New Mexico Press, 1999. This is a compilation of nearly forty Mayan Indian folktales, focusing on the Quiché-Maya of Lake Atitlán in Guatemala.

Michael Silverstone, *Rigoberta Menchu: Defending Human Rights in Guatemala.* New York: Feminist Press at the City University of New York, 1998. Written for the young-adult reader, this is an account of Rigoberta Menchú's struggle for the human rights of her people.

WORKS CONSULTED

BOOKS

Archidiocese of Guatemala, Thomas Quigley, *Never Again!* Maryknoll, NY: Orbis, 1999. Offers a firsthand account of the civil war in Guatemala.

Stephen Connely Benz, *Guatemala Journey.* Austin: University of Texas Press, 1996. Gives a good description of Guatemala's geography.

Nick Cullather and Piero Gleijeses, *Secret History: The CIA's Classified Account of Its Operations in Guatemala, 1952–1954.* Palo Alto, CA: Stanford University Press, 1999. Provides good analysis of the CIA's involvement in overthrowing the Arbenz government in 1954.

Paul J. Dosal, *Doing Business with the Dictators: A Political History of United Fruit in Guatemala, 1899–1944.* Wilmington, DE: Scholarly Resources, 1993. Gives analysis of the relationship between the United Fruit Company and the events leading up to the overthrow of the government in 1954.

Edward F. Fischer and R. McKenna Brown, eds., *Maya Cultural Activism in Guatemala.* Austin: University of Texas Press, 1997. Provides a good description of the political atmosphere in contemporary Guatemala.

Greg Grandin, *The Blood of Guatemala: A History of Race and Nation.* Durham, NC: Duke University Press, 2000. Provides a good history of the cultural and ethnic divisions that exist in Guatemala.

Jim Handy, *Gift of the Devil: A History of Guatemala.* Cambridge, MA: South End Press, 1990. This is a good general history of Guatemala.

W. George Lovell, *A Beauty That Hurts.* Austin: University of

Texas Press, 1995. Offers firsthand narratives of life in Guatemala during the civil war.

Richard Mahler, *Guatemala: Adventures in Nature.* Berkeley, CA: John Muir, 1999. Provides a valuable description of different regions of Guatemala.

Trish O'Kane, *In Focus Guatemala: A Guide to the People, Politics, and Culture.* Northampton, MA: Interlink, 2003. Provides valuable political and cultural descriptions of Guatemala.

Mark Pendergrast, *Uncommon Ground: The History of Coffee and How It Transformed Our World.* New York: Basic, 2000. Gives an explanation of the importance of coffee cultivation in Guatemala.

Richard B. Primack, David Barton Bray, Hugo A. Galletti, and Ismael Ponciano, eds., *Timber, Tourists and Temples: Conservation and Development in the Maya Forest of Belize, Guatemala, and Mexico.* Washington, DC: Island, 1997. Provides essays about the state of the Mayan culture in the contemporary world.

Maureen E. Shea, *Culture and Customs of Guatemala.* Westport, CT: Greenwood Press, 2001. Provides a comprehensive examination of the culture of Guatemala.

Stephen Schlesinger and Stephen Kinzer, *Bitter Fruit: The Story of the American Coup in Guatemala.* Cambridge, MA: Harvard University Press, 1990. Gives a history of the events leading up to the 1954 coup as well as the civil war.

David Stoll, *Rigoberta Menchú and the Story of All Poor Guatemalans.* Boulder, CO: Westview Press, 1999. Provides a valuable description of the conditions under which the Guatemalan indigenous population has lived from the civil war to the present.

Daniel Wilkenson, *Silence on the Mountain: Stories of Terror, Betrayal, and Forgetting in Guatemala.* Boston: Houghton Mifflin, 2002. Gives personal narrative accounts of Guatemala's civil war.

PERIODICALS

Robert A. Rice, "A Rich Brew from the Shade," *Américas, Organization of American States*, March/April 1998, vol. 50, no. 2, pp. 52–59.

K. Mitchel Snow, "Exposing a Heritage in Color & Light," *Américas, Organization of American States*, September/October 1998, vol. 50, no. 5, pp. 46–51.

AUDIO SOURCES

Gerry Hadden, "Guatemala Killings Prompt Call for Probe," *Morning Edition*, National Public Radio News, February 7, 2003.

———, "Election Sets Guatemala on Edge," *All Things Considered*, National Public Radio News, November 6, 2003.

INTERNET SOURCES

"Central America and the Caribbean: Guatemala," Nationmaster.com. April 2004. www.nationmaster.com/country/gt.

Mark Graffis, "Guatemala May Repeat Mayan History," June 15, 1998. www.hartford-hwp.com/archives/41/205.html.

Suzy Hansen, "The Land Where Terror Won," October 16, 2002. http://archive.salon.com/books/int/2002/10/16/wilkinson.

"Lakes," www.enjoyguatemala.com/lakes.htm.

P. Landmeier, "Banana Republic: The United Fruit Company," 1997. www.mayaparadise.com/ufc1e.htm.

Don Lotter, "The Price, Processing and Production Challenges of Growing Coffee Profitably & Sustainably in Guatemala," The New Farm, April 15, 2003. www.newfarm.org/international/guatemala/coffee.shtml.

Office of the Historian, "Foreign Relations, Guatemala, 1952–1954," U.S. Department of State. www.state.gov/r/pa/ho/frus/ike/guat/20171.htm.

Anita Snow, "Maya Indians No Longer Hide Ancient Faith Behind Catholicism," www.indians.org/welker/maya1.htm.

WEBSITES

Destination 360 (www.destination360.com/tikal/guide.htm). This site provides information on many travel destinations, including Guatemala, and provides a virtual tour of the Mayan ruins of Tikal.

Nationmaster.com (www.nationmaster.com/country/gt). This site provides valuable facts and figures about many nations, including contemporary Guatemala.

Travel for kids (http://travelforkids.com/Funtodo/Guatemala/guatemala.htm). This site provides a description of various regions of Guatemala.

The World Almanac for Kids Online (www.worldalmanac forkids.com/explore/nations/guatemala.html). This almanac provides information on many nations and includes resources for children to learn more about Guatemala.

INDEX

Picture Credits

ABOUT THE AUTHOR

Kevin Delgado was born in Torrington, Wyoming, the seventh of twelve children. He has a bachelor's degree in history and English from San Diego State University and an MFA in creative writing from New York University. He currently lives in San Diego, California, with his wife and four children.